Surviving Difficult
Church Members

Creative Leadership Series

Surviving Difficult Church Members

Robert D. Dale

Creative Leadership Series
Lyle E. Schaller, Editor

Abingdon Press / Nashville

Surviving Difficult Church Members

Copyright © 1984 by Abingdon Press

Library of Congress Cataloging in Publication Data

DALE, ROBERT D.
  Surviving difficult church members.
  (Creative leadership series)
  Includes bibliographical references.
  1. Church management. 2. Pastoral theology,
  3. Church controversies. I. Title. II. Series.
  BV652.D35   1984   253   83-25796

ISBN 0-687-40763-X (Soft Cover)

Scripture quotations unless otherwise noted are from the Revised
Standard Version Common Bible, copyright © 1973 by the Division of
Christian Education of the National Council of the Churches of Christ in
the U.S.A., and are used by permission.

MANUFACTURED BY THE PARTHENON PRESS AT
NASHVILLE, TENNESSEE, UNITED STATES OF AMERICA

Acknowledgments

Books rarely fall from the skies edited and bound. They grow layer upon layer like an onion—and sometimes cause tears like an onion too.

This book is no exception. I owe a debt of gratitude to lots of people for the ideas on these pages. I can't thank everyone, but several special persons and groups deserve public appreciation.

Thanks to conference groups and seminary classes for helping test and polish these materials. The "loneliness is . . ." and similar sections were gathered out of these settings. Thanks to the difficult church members I've worked with and the times when I've been able to be reasonably objective about my own difficult behavior. Thanks to Lyle Schaller and the publishers for their encouragement and assistance. Thanks to Mrs. Mary Lou Stephens for careful preparation of the manuscript. And thanks in advance for the helpful feedback you'll provide as you read this book.

68413

Foreword

Nearly every congregation includes a couple of members the leaders wish had joined the church across the street or down the road. These are the people nearly every member finds it difficult to get along with in a satisfying manner. Some pastors insist the church tends to attract, in disproportionately large numbers, the neurotic, the lonely, the hostile, and the maladjusted personalities.

Newcomers, as well as a substantial number of longtime members, often criticize the congregation to which they belong as "cliquish" or "run by a couple of cliques" or "filled with cliques." The members of these so-called cliques frequently respond, "Well, after all, if they want to gain a sense of belonging here, they must at least meet us halfway. We've invited them to join our group, but they never come. They just sit on the sidelines and complain about being excluded."

Occasionally one finds a church in which the monthly board meeting is always disrupted by the same person who appears to have a highly developed skill at making everyone else wish they had stayed home that night.

These are simply three of the six types of individuals identified by Bob Dale in this book. He not only identifies personality types every church leader will recognize, he also parallels these diagnostic chapters with constructive suggestions on the appropriate ministry skills for responding to the needs and demands of a variety of difficult people. Professor Dale concludes this book on a very positive note with several suggestions on how to affirm strengths and to build relationships in a constructive manner.

Many readers also will find this book to be very useful in their life at the office or in the factory or at the store, as well as in their life as a volunteer. We meet difficult people wherever we go.

This book is the fourth in the CREATIVE LEADERSHIP SERIES directed at the concerns of those who work with volunteers. The readers of this volume may want to refer to such earlier volumes as *The Care and Feeding of Volunteers* by Douglas W. Johnson or *Leading Churches through Change* by Douglas Alan Walrath or *Leadership and Conflict* by Speed Leas for ideas on survival in a world of volunteers.

Lyle E. Schaller
Yokefellow Institute
Richmond, Indiana

Contents

I

Keeping Difficult
from Becoming Impossible

"He's impossible!" "No one can get along with her!" Have you ever said or thought that about a fellow church member? Most of us have. And in saying or thinking that, we've identified a "difficult church member."

That judgment made about a member of our own congregation forces us toward two reminders. (1) All of us are "under construction." We're still growing, developing, becoming. That includes the difficult church member too. (2) Watch the difficult person who irritates us the most. He may mirror our own feared traits. As Harry Emerson Fosdick said, "Watch what people are cynical or critical about and you can soon discover what they lack."

This book is about people who can threaten congregational health. It's also about the ministry skills needed by church leaders for effectiveness with difficult church members.

Ministry to the Difficult Person

How does a congregation treat its oddball members? That's my rule of thumb test for the strength of a church's fellowship. Do we care for the mismatched members of our own congregations?

The Exodus experience left an interesting scar on Israel,

a sensitive area the nation couldn't shake. "The stranger within your gates" reminded Israel that she had been a homeless misfit within the human race. Afterwards, Israel always felt obligated to offer hospitality to the alien. How do we treat those people who belong but don't fit in comfortably? Are our churches ministering to its lovable and unlovable difficult members, our own strangers inside our own church gates?

My church experience and the testimonies of friends who are pastors and laypersons identify six difficult church members who demand but deflect ministry attempts: the lonely, the clique, the noncommunicating crazymaker, the hostile, the apathetic, and the traditionalist. These people are challenges to their own congregation's effectiveness.

The lonely church member. Whom do you think of in that category? Consider these one-word snapshots of loneliness. Withdrawn. Shy. Solitary. Forlorn. Desolate. Forsaken. Isolated. In-grown. These folks call us close—then hold us away.

The clique in the church. The in-group. The power elite. The closed cluster. The exclusive crowd. The word clique comes from the French term for "to make noise." Cliques often become noisy and create difficulties for the larger Christian fellowship.

The noncommunicating crazymaker. These folks keep relational connections from being made. Communication makes information common, enhances sharing, and exchanges meanings. The crazymaker throws everyone off stride by blocking communication patterns.

The hostile. Do you know any church members who seem to be perpetually angry? Intimidators. Menacing. Confrontational. Habitual opponents. At war with the world. As one church member announced to me, "This church will never have a unanimous vote as long as I'm a member here." His "principle" of negative actions upset constructive ministries.

The apathetic member. Indifferent. Literally "without emotion." Unconcerned. Listless. Unfeeling and emotionless. Numbness. Shrugged shoulders. What do you suppose eroded the commitment and zeal of Demas, Paul's companion (Col. 4:14; Philem. 1:24), who fell in love with the world and deserted Paul's missionary enterprises (II Tim. 4:10)? What triggered his apathy?

The traditionalist. Change resistant. The conservator. Firmly settled. Unmovable. Stationary. Those who long for a romanticized past. Remember the Luddites? They were Britons who in the 1800s rioted against time-saving machines and tried to make the clock stand still. They dug in against the future, idolizing a hallowed history.

The lonely and the clique hold a characteristic in common. They're non-connectors. They relate selectively—if at all. The crazymaker and the hostile also share a common trait; they foul up communication. And the apathetic and traditional church members have the same characteristic; they are uncommitted.

Those Difficult Church Members

Every idea has its own pilgrimage: a beginning, a path it travels, and a goal. Here's how this material unfolded.

> *Genesis: how I got interested in ministering to difficult church members.*

Churches are made up of all kinds of people. I've discovered the largest and smallest persons in the world in

13

the church. Saints and martyrs sit side by side on our pews with those who hate and cheat and sow division. Let me illustrate the mixed nature of the church. I remember historian Vernon Parrington's story about the banker who taught Sunday school early each Sunday morning and then while he sat in worship plotted whom he would cheat the next day. Further, C. S. Lewis' *Great Divorce* parable describes a thriving congregation in hell. It's a going concern. It just isn't going anywhere near the kingdom of God. Aren't most local churches collections of great souls and difficult members?

By and large, congregations don't choose their members. People volunteer to join the church of their preference. Inevitably, most congregations have within them the full range of personality types and human behaviors. Ministry implies a covenant to care for all members of a congregation. That's a real challenge for both lay members and pastors. How can you minister effectively to persons who are difficult to relate to under the best of circumstances?

Pastors report that certain types of members are special ministry challenges. For five years, I led pastors' seminars all across the United States. During that time I listened carefully to pastors as they described the persons who were most difficult for them to relate to and to treat in the spirit of Christ. Their list centered around the six persons or groups I've already mentioned.

The difficult church member isn't always "them." In the words of the "prophet" Pogo, "We have met the enemy and they are us!" Difficult church members aren't psychopaths, sociopaths, the deviant, or the disordered; they are folks like us. In fact, they are us at many points. Those who "hook" us may reflect our threatening shadows. The Germans call these shadows *doppelgangers*, our doubles. You and I may relate poorly to some other fellow church members because they possess characteristics we fear we may acquire.

Exodus: mapping the difficult church member.

I'm not thinking of the emotionally imbalanced person when I use the phrase "the difficult church member." I'm thinking of the congregational mismatch, the square peg in the round hole. These folks have a barb, a rough spot, an abrasive characteristic. They probably rub many other persons the wrong way. Like oil and water, they don't mix or fit in well with the majority of the congregation. They are out-of-step in some way or out-of-sync on some issue. While "fit" is a two-way street, the difficult church member is a misfit within his congregation in some obvious way.

The difficult church member usually doesn't realize he's out-of-step. Remember the old story about the proud mother who thought every other member of the marching band was out-of-step except her Johnny? Often difficult members aren't fully conscious of the problems they create.

Difficult church members control others with their behavior. They keep those who try to deal with them preoccupied, off balance. Just when you think you have them and the situation mastered, the difficult person changes the pace of interaction with an emotional feint. Like a hard throwing baseball pitcher, who without warning slips in a big, slow, tantalizing curve, we are kept uncertain about what to expect next.

Gospels: ministering effectively to difficult church members.

The guide for human relations in the church is the Golden Rule of Jesus (Matt. 7:12). Our goal in ministry is to treat everyone alike and just the way we'd like to be cared for. Remember the observation of Goethe: "Treat people as if they were what they ought to be and you help them to become what they are capable of being."

Coping with the difficult person must not become manipulation. We accept them, warts and all. We need their spiritual gifts for the church's work. Our strategy is to love them, understand them, and help them get back in balance so the church can minister more effectively.

Control: the common need

Controlling our lives is a universal need. While it isn't our only need, we all want to feel a measure of control over our lives—especially in groups. Difficult church members control others by their behavior either unconsciously or deliberately.[1] How do our six difficult member types control their fellow church members?

The lonely frustrate their congregations with "help me—I need you" signals coupled with "but stay at arm's length" behavior. Their control shows itself in two dimensions. They control others' attempts to establish friendships. They also control other church members by creating a guilty conscience in those who try unsuccessfully to reach out to them.

Cliques influence their congregations by controlling the climate of their church for good or ill. Some cliques signal heavy weather for their churches; their very presence indicates storm clouds. They are gathering for protection,

16

war, or revenge. Other cliques are friendlier and exist to give their members needed information or status.

Crazymakers control relational agendas by selective attention and by confusing interpersonal communication patterns and channels. They cause uncertainty and, therefore, keep the leverage of the relationship in their hands.

Hostile members control us by being "willing to be bad." Their aggressiveness, outspokenness, and belligerence set the emotional tone of relationships and groups. When we avoid conflict or demonstrate discomfort with conflict, the hostile member has a measure of control over us.

The apathetic member controls his church in at least three ways. He doesn't invest himself in support of the mission or goals of the congregation. He doesn't take the risks necessary for faith in action. He splits the church's energy focus between ministry to "them out there" and "us in here."

Traditionalists control the future of their congregations by idolizing the past. Their resistance to change blocks all but the most obvious and acute changes, and, thereby, controls the ministry agendas of their churches.

A Map for This Book

This book is made up of paired chapters—one chapter describing a difficult church member coupled with a second chapter on the ministry skills necessary for effective congregational work with that personality type. "Who" is linked to "how." Description is followed by prescription.

Two reminders: "He" is used generically since difficult persons are both male and female. Persons and events mentioned in this book have been disguised.

Read on with the hope of gaining insight and skills for making your own church healthier, happier, and more productive.

II

Loneliness:
America's Number One Disease

Loneliness infects more Americans than any other disease. Rich and poor. Young and old. Famous and anonymous. Each of us at some time feels a not-at-homeness.

We all know the problem from personal experience. Thomas Wolfe described himself as "a mad fellow who made loneliness his mistress." America's premier advice givers, twins Abigail Van Buren and Ann Landers, place loneliness as one of the top ten concerns of their readers. I'll go one step further: loneliness was the most common problem I encountered in the congregations I pastored. In the Bible, Job referred to the jackal as his brother (Job 30:29). He had reached a state in life where his only ally was a beast who wanted him dead so it could eat his rotting carcass.

Needed: A Friend

Several years ago a Baptist pastor from South Carolina asked his congregation to tell him the role they needed most from him. Predictable words like "preacher," "counselor," and "worship leader" cropped up often. But to this pastor's surprise, the majority of the members of his church needed him most as "friend." Friendship is the foundation for ministry. A commitment to Christian friendship, then, is a basic step toward ministering to the lonely members of our churches.

Lonely persons suffer from a relational deficiency. They aren't alone necessarily, but they feel no one really knows them. Loneliness is more than aloneness. It's a special kind of aloneness and is different from solitude.

Solitary Isn't Lonely

Solitariness and loneliness are related but different experiences. You can undergo solitude without loneliness. Alfred North Whitehead, the philosopher, claimed that religion is what you do with your solitariness. Whitehead was emphatic in asserting that "if you are never solitary, you are never religious . . ."[1] If Whitehead is right, how we respond to our lonely times may deepen our faith.

How is solitariness distinct from loneliness? Solitariness is the state of being alone; it's the external condition when no one else is physically present. Loneliness is being destitute of friendly relationships; it's both an internal and an external condition since you may be in a crowd and still feel lonely.

Feeling solitude means being by yourself; no one is there with you; you're remote from others. Feeling lonely means no one is responsive to you; no one cares for or sympathizes with you; you are emotionally cut off from others.

Did Jesus experience solitude? Loneliness? Both? I suspect he felt both solitude and loneliness at times. For example, Jesus regularly retreated for rest and refreshment. On the other hand, on the cross he apparently felt abandoned: "My God, my God, why hast thou forsaken me?" (Mark 15:34).

A poet, living alone in the Maine woods, noted "the worst part of what I experience is loneliness. The best part of what I experience is solitude."[2]

Lonely Is . . .

When were you loneliest? Can you pinpoint a time when you felt totally isolated? For some of my friends, lonely is . . .

- The night before surgery.
- Homecoming without a date.
- Hearing your spouse say, "I don't love you any more. I'm leaving you."
- Sunday afternoon in a college dorm.
- When it's time to turn out the light and go to sleep in a strange motel room in an unfamiliar town.
- Solitary confinement.
- When the home nest is empty after your children are grown.
- Being airborne in a plane with mechanical difficulties.
- Finding yourself in a foreign culture where no one speaks your language.
- Being chosen last on the teams for playground games.
- When you feel the whole world's down on you.
- Eating by yourself.
- When no one understands you, and they don't even try.
- Having a baby when your family is far away.
- Setting expectations for yourself too high and failing.
- Having young ideas in an old church.
- Getting pressure from your family and others to get married.
- Finding out your parents have separated.
- Visiting a church and feeling unwelcomed.

- When your child dies.
- Having an alcoholic father who doesn't come home.
- A broken engagement.
- Being in a military command position when your men's lives are at stake.
- Taking an unpopular point of view, which your conscience forces you to hold onto.
- Riding a bicycle built for two—alone.
- Finding the roses you sent aren't the only ones she got.
- Being the only one who can't swim when you and your friends go swimming.
- Being a single parent.
- Facing the death of a loved one.
- Being overdrawn at the bank and realizing it's two weeks until payday.
- Going to a movie by yourself.
- Making the final "out" when your team is one run behind.
- A busy signal on the phone.
- Going blank on a final exam.
- Being made fun of.
- Being white in Spanish Harlem.
- Going home by yourself after a divorce hearing.
- Being in an emergency room all by yourself.
- When you can't pray.
- The first night at boot camp.
- Being lost.
- A stormy midnight in Savannah with a broken alternator belt . . . seven hours from anyone who knows your name . . . with no money except a two-party check no one will cash . . . after just having broken up with your girl friend . . . and not knowing where your parents' new home is in Florida or how to get there.

The Case of Lonely Leo

All of us feel lonely at times. But some folks raise loneliness to an art form. Leo is a case in point. He repels anyone who approaches him while all the time calling out for contact.

Leo is a middle-aged husband and father. I met him first over the telephone. It was an unforgettable call—for one thing, the conversation lasted two hours. I had just become his pastor and was trying to get acquainted with all the members of my congregation. So the call was welcomed. Actually, Leo had called my associate since I hadn't met him yet. Van, my associate, had shown concern for Leo for several years before my arrival. I had stuck my head into Van's office to invite him to lunch. He waved me in. I waited while he nodded and said "uh-huh" several times. Finally, Van said, "I know Bob would like to hear about that." With that Van handed me the phone and left for lunch!

I wasn't quite sure what was going on, but after a brief introduction, Leo seized the moment and started telling me all his troubles. Leo's conversation was a litany of woes—rambling and random. He leaped from subject to subject with the words jumbling and tumbling out in a torrent. Rarely did I get a word wedged in—and then only when I interrupted him. I felt captured by a person I didn't really know yet. Then my chance to escape arrived. Van returned from lunch. I broke in on Leo's monologue with "I know Van will be interested to hear about that." Then I handed Van the receiver and went to lunch! That original call signaled how much in need Leo was. He was desperately lonely but drove away those who were willing to try to break through his isolation.

Soon I visited Leo's family in their home—a small wooden duplex. In poor health, he was rarely able to go out. His telephone provided most of his contact with the outside world. His wife, a small, defiant woman, and their rebellious teenage son spent no more time at home than was absolutely necessary. Leo was cut off from people.

One day he called my study and in a breathless conspiratorial voice said, "I saw her today!" I wondered if I should ask but did anyway. "Her?" "Yes. Today I saw the black cat!" Again I wondered if I was going to hate myself for inquiring, "the black cat?" "Oh, yes. Today I saw the black cat—the one that carries the family curse!" Leo felt that his family had been cursed and that the curse was passed down generation by generation when the cat touched a member of the next generation. Leo was vastly relieved that he had been able to scurry across a shopping center parking lot to the safety of his car.

The chilling proof of Leo's loneliness occurred every winter. Almost on schedule when the weather was at its worst, Leo's legs would become infected, and he would be hospitalized under the threat of amputation. So again into the hospital he would go—and enjoy every moment of being cared for and touched and talked to and bathed. The doctors, nurses, and I agreed: while Leo's medical condition was serious, his real illness was loneliness. No one could break through his shell. If Leo was cursed, his personal demon was falling completely into the grip of that universal human condition, loneliness.

Loneliness May Be Dangerous to Your Health

Loneliness kills. At least that's the view of James J. Lynch. A specialist in psychosomatic medicine at the

University of Maryland Medical School, Lynch observes that isolation and the breaking down of human ties erode your health. For example, folks who are widowed and divorced are more apt to undergo a health breakdown. Boston Irishmen have more heart disease than their family members who didn't immigrate. Nevada records a higher coronary death rate than Utah, a difference which relates to freewheeling life-styles in contrast to a stable Mormon emphasis on family. Lynch's conclusion? That community and family relationships improve your health.

Lynch stresses the importance of touch—both in the physician's bedside manner and in the contact patients have with hospital visitors. We need love and human contact. Lynch claims loneliness can literally break your heart. He asserts that "there is a biological basis for our need to form loving human relationships. If we fail to fulfill that need, our health is in peril."[3] The church has an important opportunity to confront loneliness.

Fellowship: The Church's Response to Loneliness

The Bible uses an entire family of "koinon" words to describe the fellowship in Christ, which dispels loneliness. In the New Testament alone, the "koinon" group words appear about fifty times. Savor these biblical ideas and see if you don't find them chasing "the lonelies" away. Companion. Partaker. Communion. In common. Shares with. Partnership. Joined together. Bound together.

Paul speaks often of fellowship and views it in two dimensions. First, fellowship has a vertical relationship. We who have put our faith in Christ have a share in him and in his benefits. Paul's letters to the churches overflow with compound verbs about our relationship to Christ—alive with, crucified with, buried with, glorified with, raised with, reigning with. All with Christ. We share in Christ. We are not alone.

Second, fellowship has a horizontal relationship too. We also share together with other Christians. Because of Christ, we are fellow servants, fellow workers, and fellow citizens. Again, loneliness is dispelled by our common ties through Christ.

Paul's "body of Christ" metaphor links our common ties with Christ and his followers. The body of Christ is unified or bound together by Christ; yet we are different in what we give to the body individually. "For as in one body we have many members, and all the members do not have the same function, so we, though many, are one body in Christ, and individually members one of another" (Rom. 12:4-5). Together in Christ. Together with each other. Not lonely.

III

Making Friends in Christ's Name

Friendships are the bridges to ministry. Especially for the lonely. I'm intrigued by the way Jesus formed a relationship with Zacchaeus. I suspect Zacchaeus was hungry for a quality relationship. Consider his situation. Political turncoat. A cheat. Excluded from the synagogue. His family cut off from social ties. Then Jesus called Zacchaeus by name, initiated a relationship, and went home with Zacchaeus. No wonder Zacchaeus' life was revolutionized! This encounter challenges us to make friends in Christ's name. Loneliness is dispelled, and faith is enriched by our Christian network.

A Model of Loneliness

Who are the top candidates for loneliness? Research shows that women, the poor, and the divorced or widowed are most likely to experience loneliness. They are apt to make the painful discovery that the lonely person lacks a particular type of relationship.

A friend of mine told me about the day his relational network collapsed. When he arrived at home after work, his wife announced, "Fred, I'm leaving you" (Loss #1), "and I'm taking our daughters with me too" (Loss #2).

His in-laws sided with his ex-wife (Loss #3). His church excluded him from his leadership posts (Loss #4). Fred's parents didn't understand or know how to be supportive (Loss #5). His workmates didn't rally around either, except for the custodian in Fred's office. Every major relationship Fred had before those fatal words, "I'm leaving you," were heard dissolved almost immediately. Fred claims he kept his sanity that winter by remodeling a small house he moved into.

Fred's experience is repeated often in other's lives. Robert Weiss and his fellow researchers have discovered two types of loneliness in the Freds of the world.[1]

"Social isolation" is the lack of a network of peers. This "cloud of witnesses" is ordinarily made up of friends, fellow workers, neighbors, kinsmen, hobbyists of like interests, fellow club members, and, importantly for our purposes, church members. A social network is needed by each one of us. However, multiplying our social relationships can't offset the lack of more significant and deeper relationships. Social isolation is lessened by putting ourselves into settings in which acceptance by others is made easier simply because we're near others.

"Emotional isolation" is the lack of or the loss of a truly intimate tie. Intimate relationships link us to parents, spouses, our children, a counselor, and our pastor. Relationships of this intensity are necessary to all.

Jesus gathered a large cluster of disciples, and they provided him with a buffer against social isolation. The so-called "inner circle" made up of Peter, James, and John was apparently his primary emotional support system. It is significant that the Twelve were called for ministry and "to be with him" (Mark 3:14-15).

A Congregational Strategy for Ministering to Lonely Persons

How can healthy churches support their own difficult and lonely members? Five initiatives help cope with loneliness.

- *Self-valuing: first line of defense against loneliness*

According to Hritzuk, total loneliness grows out of a lack of love for yourself (as well as an inability to establish meaningful relationships with others).[2] The person who doesn't value himself is a prime candidate for loneliness.

Jesus' Great Commandment contains an often overlooked order: "You shall love the Lord your God with all . . . you shall love your neighbor *as yourself*' (Matt. 22:37-39). Healthy self-regard is the basis for relating to God and others. No ministry of the church to lonely persons is more fundamental than helping them believe they are worthy of the friendship of others. After all, since persons are created in the image of God and recreated or made new by Christ, sin is overcome and realistic self-valuing is possible.

- *Energy: someone has to make the first move*

Friendships don't develop instantly or grow automatically. Relationships usually are rooted in initiative, risk, and effort. Someone has to make the first move every day. Someone chooses to offer friendly help.

Take the case of Betsy Olive as an example.[3] She's a professional friend, a social worker, and she spends lots of energy helping her friends. During a recent period of bitter winter weather, Mrs. Olive became concerned for K. T., a client so mentally marginal that he might not realize how cold the temperature was until he was frozen. After a day of searching, she saw K. T. lying in a field beside some smoking twigs. He was only napping. Mrs. Olive delivered K. T. to a relative's warm house. Today she finds he has disappeared again. He isn't at his sister's home. He isn't at his home—the roof has caved in under the weight of snow. After several blind alley leads she finally locates K. T., who has found work on a man's farm.

Betsy Olive is direct with her client. Do you have socks on? Go by the church and pick up some more clothes. Are you taking your medicine? No more sleeping in that field! K. T. smiles and nods agreement. Then Mrs. Olive adds the clincher: "I'll never go away, K. T., never go away." Her willingness to maintain this friendship is virtually endless.

Friendships around the church don't thrive on autopilot. Good relationships bear the marks of loving effort. Lonely persons need to receive a clear message from at least some members of the church: "We'll never go away!"

- *Pacing: the seasons of friendship*

If you try to force a rose bud into full bloom instantly, you only succeed in ruining the flower. Its petals are bruised and broken. The same tragedy happens in friendships when we ignore the crucial relationship building dimension of timing.

A young friend of mine hasn't developed a sense of relational pacing yet. He falls in love and wants to get married on the first date every time he meets a new girl. The girl usually enjoys his undivided attention for about three days, and then she begins to feel smothered. She tries to create some distance and buy some time. He only pursues harder. She finally has to drop him. He's hurt and confused. Then another girl catches his eye, and the cycle repeats itself.

New relationships must be tenderly nurtured. A budding friendship usually involves sharing a lot of no-risk or low-risk information about you, your background, and your family. Then, as the relationship deepens and broadens, more and more personal disclosures can be shared without threatening the friendship or inviting ridicule.

A communications professor uses a process of telling high-risk secrets to sensitize his students to the pacing factor in building friendships.[4] He asks his students to write their most closely guarded secrets on note cards. He then collects the cards and redistributes them. The secrets are read aloud and reacted to. This process usually liberates the secret-holders from their fears. They find others have had similar fears and are, therefore, understanding of them. For instance, a Vietnam veteran was comforted when he found his classmates could identify with his secret: he had protected himself during a mortar attack by pulling the body of a dead soldier over himself.

Research indicates that sex-related secrets both trouble people most and are riskiest to tell. Incest, institutionalization for mental illness, venereal disease, homosexual tendencies, drug abuse, suicidal thoughts, shoplifting, and cheating are the highest ranking risky secrets. Telling this kind of secret too soon can destroy relationships. Sensitivity to timing helps you know when a friendship can bear high-risk sharing.

The process of Christian nurture provides congregations a parallel to relational pacing. We aren't fully mature in Christ instantly. Our faith pilgrimage leads us steadily from the baby food of spiritual infancy to the solid nourishment of Christian maturity. A commitment to encouraging the seasons of our long-term spiritual journey reminds us that friendships for ministry must also be carefully paced.

A special relational opportunity in the church is ministry to others during a crisis. The emergency circumstances create an atmosphere in which the pace of friendship is accelerated and the intensity is deepened.

- *Compatible Interests: an essential ingredient*

Opposites do attract initially. But lasting friendships revolve around common interests in part. People who are similar in significant ways form longer-term relationships.

Churches and communities have established a range of situational groups around common concerns: parents without partners, divorce support groups, and newcomer groups. A Baptist church in Georgia with an older membership has formed a grief support group providing information and encouragement for persons navigating that difficult life passage. A city in Kansas developed a "ring-a-day" program of daily telephone contacts for elderly and homebound citizens. A programming possibility, then, for congregations wishing to reach out to the lonely is to establish contact groups around issues of mutual needs.

- *Accessibility: the search for comfortable settings*

Where do lonely people find others to befriend and to be befriended by? A lot of places—clubs, shopping centers, restaurants, doctor's offices, at work. Churches can host a variety of groups and provide a setting for lonely persons to meet and become acquainted with a minimum of pressure. Accessibility to comfortable settings provides people with a point of contact.

One congregation started a group for those who were formerly married. The first session drew six persons. But within a few months eighty widows/widowers and divorcees were meeting every other week. The church staff served as hosts and program resource persons. Topics discussed ranged from religious to emotional to financial issues. One session each month was a potluck dinner. Occasionally the group took all of their children to the park for a mass picnic and ballgame. (It was interesting to watch how much these children of one-parent families were "momma-ed" and "daddy-ed" and grandparented in this relaxed setting. The real parents enjoyed the support and felt some of their parenting demands were lessened for a few hours.)

Coping with Personal Loneliness

Sometimes we who are trying to help the lonely person experience loneliness ourselves. Several common strategies help us break through our times of isolation.

- Acceptance of yourself provides a foundation for building (new) relationships. Self-confidence is necessary for relating; we give something to each other when we share friendship.
- Allow others to come to your rescue. Let your needs be known. Be accessible to others.
- Actively seek out people. Begin with folks you know already—friends from the past. Make the first move.
- Share your feelings with a supportive person. Allow yourself to become vulnerable.

- Accept friendship.
- Loneliness is a choice. It can't be blamed totally on others. Take responsibility for ending your isolation. Face your fears about change and rejection.

Risking and Relating

Relationships are risky. When we get close to others, we can help and be helped or hurt and be hurt. In ministry, there is always the chance of being rejected or used. But the risk is worth taking because relationships are the bridges for ministry.

Risk and relationships go hand-in-hand. Even the animals in children's books have learned that valuable lesson. Said the Skin Horse to the Velveteen Rabbit about becoming real:

"It doesn't happen all at once . . . You become. It takes a long time. That's why it doesn't often happen to people
  who break easily,
  or have sharp edges,
  who have to be carefully kept.
Generally, by the time you are Real,
  most of your hair has been loved off,
and your eyes drop out
  and you get loose in the joints
  and very shabby.
But these things don't matter at all,
  because once you are Real
  you can't be ugly,
  except to people who don't understand."[5]
There's beauty in friendship. And relationships provide us with the foundation for Christian ministry.

IV

Insecurity at Work:
Cliques in Control

Billy Martin was once interviewed about what made him a successful manager of a professional baseball team. He replied that on every team there are five players who love you, five who hate you, and fifteen who simply want to play ball.

"Being a successful manager," he continued, "is to keep the five who hate you away from the other twenty."

That's a pretty good formula for keeping a vocal clique from controlling the organizational climate of a church too.

Cliques: Group Challenge to Ministry

Humans are social creatures. We have a deep need to belong, to be accepted by others. Our natural need to be with others is shown by joining clubs, hobby groups, community activities, sports teams, and the church. By and large, we join groups for two reasons: (1) we like persons in the group and join to be with them, and (2) we believe in the goals of the group and invest in the common cause.

Beyond belonging

Christians gathered into groups can be a good news-bad news story. It's good news indeed when we experience the communion or oneness defining the fellowship of believers. The network of believers is very good news.

However, some church groups can be bad news too. Christians don't always settle for belonging to God's larger family. We may press on to create an exclusive group, an "in crowd," a clique. And for every "in crowd" there must be an "out group" to identify against for protection or control. We narrow our social circles drastically when we decide there's no prestige in belonging to the human race or the wider fellowship of believers. The Pharisees of the New Testament offer a prime example of how a noble group can narrow itself into exclusiveness and doctrinaire rigidity. Like the Pharisees, we create cliques to deal with our insecurities and to maintain control within the wider group.

Historically, closed groups have needed other groups to resist. In the Old Testament, the chosen people of Israel differentiated themselves from "the nations." During the Crusades a Christian leader speculated that God's only reason for creating Moslems was in order to fill up hell.

Cliques I have known and loved

"In" versus "out"—it is one predictable way we humans try to control our destinies, meet our belonging needs, and achieve an identity. Some cliques are healthy, in spite of being exclusive groups. For example, support groups are deliberately structured cliques.

The result of these closed groups is positive ministry. Other examples of useful exclusive groups include prayer groups, Sunday school classes that include newcomers gladly, and church committees that do their work effectively without forgetting the broader goals of the larger congregation.

Cliques I have known and hated

The healthy human concern that binds us together in supportive groups, loving families, and caring congregations—when overdone—fosters destructive, even extremist, groups. Think of the groups you are part of as a continuum with each type of group on the continuum as one response to feelings of insecurity.[1]

At one end of the continuum is the feeling of being ill-at-ease, typical of some social settings—like the teenager without social confidence, the commoner among royalty, or the stranger in a new group. In such situations we need to have the ice broken and to feel welcomed. Low-level insecurity, experienced as personal discomfort in groups, usually leads to new friendships within the group.

Toward the middle of the continuum, insecurity produces cliques. When the healthy need to belong is satisfied by the unhealthy desire to exclude, a closed group forms. Like the Pharisees, who called themselves "the separated ones," we begin to define our own "in-ness" by others' "out-ness." We see life as a series of contrasts. Superior versus inferior. Right versus wrong. Male versus female. Young versus old. The possible polarities are almost endless.

What comes beyond belonging and exclusion? At the far end of the continuum lurks eradication. The extremist group is the ultimate diseased clique. When a group's reaction to insecurity is threat, an extremist group emerges. Then insecurity is structured into ideology. To wipe out other groups becomes the extremist's tactic. The Proverbist described the irrationality of the extremist as fleeing "when no one pursues" (Prov. 28:1).

Extremist groups, the ultimate cliques, take on several predictable characteristics. (1) The extremist clique blames others because they need to identify their enemies. (2) Extremist cliques hate without feeling and accuse without emotion. Extremists adopt an impersonal prejudice that sees their enemies as subhuman. (3) The extremist clique is authoritarian, inflexible, ideological, and values toughness. (4) The extremist clique demands a "they" and depends on the gang or cult group. (5) The extremist clique draws information from a narrow spectrum in order to support its own ideas. (6) The extremist clique labels others by rumor and distortion.

Unfortunately, religion is a fertile seedbed for extremist cliques. Religion, like politics, money, and sex, is a "value rich" area of life. People feel strongly about matters of faith—so strongly at times that we aren't aware of our own blindspots. Cliques with a religious veneer are difficult to deal with because the positions taken are defended by narrow theological stances.

A Clique Is . . .

Edward R. Morrow asked the poet Carl Sandburg in a televised interview, "What is the most detestable word in the English language?" Sandburg quickly spat out, "EX-X-X-clusive!" The attitude of elitism is detestable in any setting. But in the church exclusivism is inexcusable.

What, exactly, is a clique? The dictionary defines a clique as a small, exclusive group or social circle. Each of us knows the feeling of being shut out of some group. On the other hand, each of us has been part of a group that has excluded others. How do you feel when you encounter a clique?

In straightforward terms, a clique is . . .

- A group with its own jargon and "in" jokes.
- An expression of conditional acceptance.
- People with a common dress code.
- A loyal support group.
- Fun—if you belong.
- A group in which individuality is submerged.
- A "single cell" group, like a tiny, one-family church.
- Painful—if you're excluded.
- Fraternities, sororities, and some Sunday school classes.
- An escape from a few of life's realities.
- A group that makes others invisible.
- An all-male or all-female committee.
- Those who agree on what those on the outside disagree on.
- People in the same profession.
- Pastors who don't associate with laypersons.
- A board that perpetuates itself by selecting its own members.
- Realizing you have power.
- A group with a monopoly on its members' time and loyalties.
- Isolation from others outside the group.
- A group that provides belonging, identity, and protection.
- A closed system.
- A group of people with mutual interests.
- More an organism than an organization.

- Good as long as you belong.
- A potent weapon.
- A political reality.
- Potentially constructive or potentially destructive.

Metaphorically, a clique is . . .

- Me, my spouse, and our kids.
- Being the only one in the room who isn't wearing an Izod shirt!
- The Beta Club when you don't have a *B* average.
- A group of people who change the subject when an outsider comes along.
- An athletic squad—and then only the starters.
- The group that sits in pew #4 every Sunday.
- What a pastor should stay out of!
- A team you're not chosen for.
- Singles in a married class.
- A door that only opens from the inside.
- A prayer group who turn their warm side to each other and their cold side to me.

The Case of the Congregational Border Clash

Church cliques form around a variety of issues—family ties, favorite doctrines, friendship networks, work relationships, and common causes. Several years ago my family joined a Baptist church in Phoenix, Arizona. Like many of the fast-growing, southwestern cities, Phoenix is populated largely by persons who grew up some place else. Our new church reflected the "immigrant" makeup of Phoenix. A sizable group within the congregation had grown up in Texas churches. This "Texas Club" knew exactly how Baptist churches operate. Another large group of members was from Oklahoma. The "Oklahoma Club" also knew exactly how Baptists act and what we believe; but the Oklahomans didn't agree with the Texans. An "Ohio Club" was also in our church. From their point of view neither the Texans nor the Oklahomans really understood how to be Baptists. Finally, the remainder of the membership was relegated to the "Not-Texas-or-Oklahoma-or-Ohio Club" who had several other ideas about how Baptists should "do church." When the church tried to make decisions or plan programs, we disagreed and tended to ally along regional lines. The cliques in our congregation took on the flavor of border clashes. The need to decide church directions often led to controlling actions by the various cliques.

But congregations have a healthier pattern for group life than cliques. The Bible's word for an open, productive congregation is "ecclesia."

Ecclesia: Church As an Open Group

When the early Christians used the word ecclesia to refer to the church, they reminded believers in later generations of key dimensions of church life. The church is people, not place. The church is persons, not some single individual. The church is mission, not self service. The church is inclusive, not exclusive. Christ's church is open, not a closed clique.

In the Old Testament, the "assembly" was either a call to arms for the military or a summons to a town meeting for citizens. Throughout the Old Testament, ecclesia retained its "people flavor"—especially the messianic people of God. That flavor made ecclesia a natural idea for the early

41

Christian community to use in describing itself. Referring to both local congregations and to the wider church, ecclesia is the assembly of persons who are God's through Christ. The church is always militant, expanding, and open.

The people gathered around God because of Christ know something special about the church—it is Christ's, not ours. A pastor friend of mine was once caught between his convictions and his culture. It was the mid-1950s in Little Rock, Arkansas; President Eisenhower had sent in the military to integrate Central High School. My friend took a moderate stance on the race issue; but his position was too progressive for many of his members, and he watched his congregation shrink by over half. His soul-searching over the pain that came to that congregation during the racial crisis led him to one truth, which sustained him and the remnant of the congregation: the church is Christ's, not ours. Therefore, the church is Christ's to open or close. Only his choice, never ours. Ultimately, control of congregations is in Christ's hands.

V

Keeping the Glue from Becoming Too Sticky

Congregational groups cluster around similar interests. That's natural. But the glue of like concerns can get too sticky.

The Glue for Groups—Cohesion

Without the glue of cohesion, groups fragment into a thousand pieces. Some of those pieces become cliques.

Cohesion describes the degree of belonging and the level of attachment in a group. Cohesion measures the importance members have for the group. More importantly, cohesion determines the forces acting on members to keep them in the group.

Several questions uncover some basic clues to group cohesion. How often is "we" used in our group? Is the rate of absenteeism low? Do we cooperate or compete? Do we have a participative atmosphere in group decision making? Can we set group directions by discussion and consensus rather than by debate and voting? Do we like each other?

Obviously, the healthy group is cohesive. Cohesion is essential for any group to exist and to function well. The catch comes when the motive for working at cohesion is group control. When control becomes the glue for the group, a clique has evolved, and the group's health is at stake.

Stronger Than Goals

Congregations deliberately set ministry goals and organize themselves to carry out those goals. That's called formal organization.

But that's only one side to the organizational coin. On the other side is the kind of organization that emerges out of spontaneous attempts of members to meet their personal needs. To illustrate, when the need to know exceeds church newsletters and bulletin boards, a "grapevine" develops. When members feel threatened and left out of decisions, an "underground" emerges. In many cases the informal needs of a church are stronger than its formal.

In format a clique looks like any other small group in the church. But cliques are usually more cohesive than ordinary groups. Emotion is the special feature of a clique; a clique is as strong as the emotion binding it together. Common interests and ties provide the launching pad for cliques, and those common ties—family relationships, a favorite ministry issue, a special doctrinal perspective, fellow old-timers, recent members, the choir, the youth group—are as varied as individual personality itself.

The formal organization and its goals can be "managed" by church leaders. In contrast, the informal organization and its group needs must be lovingly tended. The grapevine needs cultivating. The underground needs reassuring. So the effective church leader works with the cliques of his congregation.

Seeds for Budding Cliques

Cliques grow from a myriad of reasons. Note some occasions when cliques are planted and some suggestions for coping with them.

Cliques and group stage: when do cliques form?

Groups move through a life cycle.[1] New or restructured groups move through a maturation process of several observable stages. Some of these stages are more apt to develop cliques than the others.

At the "infancy" stage, the group depends on the leader. Members raise their hands for permission to speak. They look at the leader even though they are talking to other group members. They watch the leader expectantly and wait for the leader to act. Group infancy is a dependency stage.

The "child" stage depicts the child's resistance to freedom. Sometimes freedom frightens groups, and they demand authoritarian leadership. The child wants, yet fears, the room to launch out. Like the youngster who goes to the schoolroom door on the first day of kindergarten and then begs, "Don't leave me, Mommy!" the young group resists its opportunity for freedom.

The "adolescent" stage is marked by rebellion and counterdependence. Freedom finally takes root here. The group begins to believe in itself. Rules and procedures emerge. A leadership struggle often occurs, and the designated leader may be rejected. Like the teenager who is cutting the apron strings, the group is beginning to experiment with assuming responsibility for its own life.

Independence characterizes the "collegiate" stage. Playfulness—even giddiness—is typical of the college student who leaves home, throws off his parents' rules and life-style, and "lives it up" for a time. The trigger for this stage may be a group decision that runs counter to the leader's position and symbolizes the group's readiness to celebrate its newfound freedom.

The "adult" stage yields interdependence. Now the group and leader reunite, combine resources, and contribute to group life and goal attainment. Usually shared leadership emerges and group morale rises.

When are cliques apt to form? In general, cliques are more apt to develop during the more dependent stages of group life. (1) During the infancy or child stages, the controlling leader may be seduced by the group's dependency and freeze the group at a dependent level. The Jonestown massacre reminds us of a terrifying example of personality cults, which occur in some dependent groups. (2) At mid-life, groups may let independence go to their heads, close off their boundaries, and defend their little corner of the congregation's life.

Preventing cliques calls for church leaders to concentrate on team building. New groups can be guided toward teamwork, greater interdependence, and more stable relationships.

Leader style: some cliques are made, not born

Cliques are more apt to form when the group's leader uses either a domineering or a completely "hands-off" style. Leader styles have a "ripple effect." They elicit a response from followers—that's the whole point of leadership. However, the reaction we get as leaders isn't always the one we hoped for. Kurt Lewin saw this result in some of his early research on authoritarian, democratic, and laissez-faire ("hands off") leaders. Lewin described leader style as the atmosphere setter in group life.[2]

Several implications grow out of this observation. (1) Leader-led cliques emerge when the leader insists that his goals must become the predominant congregational goals. If his force of personality is charismatic enough and the followers are dependent enough, a cult-like clique may form. (2) When dictatorial leaders constantly pressure followers, an "underground" is apt to develop for the protection of the members. (3) At the other extreme of the leadership spectrum, a laissez-faire, or path of least resistance, leader allows a vacuum to develop. In this low initiative or no initiative atmosphere, special interest groups or one-issue cliques may begin coming out of the woodwork.

From a leadership viewpoint, a participative leader style, which shares leadership throughout the congregation, gives more members a larger stake in church goal setting. This approach to leadership helps prevent cliques from forming initially and from later controlling the congregational climate.

Shifting control: when decisions must be shared

Cliques are more prevalent in situations where control is shifting. Control is a natural issue in group life. That is, each of us needs to feel some measure of influence.

Practically, most church groups aren't too tough to join. In churches we can usually feel included without getting pushy. It's the next level of group personality that gets sticky. The crunch occurs when the power structure is threatened. Here's how it happens.

Many congregations are good at outreach, evangelism, and incorporating persons into the outer circles of the fellowship. What happens, though, when new members vie with old ones for central leadership posts? Then the congregation freezes up and falls into power struggles. This tug-of-war is especially difficult for fast growing congregations who experience tension in assimilating new members into the planning and decision making processes of the church.

The control needs of groups and their members suggest several guidelines for guarding church health. (1) Power cliques revolve around the need to get in and stay in control. Where there is a lessened need for control or protection or information, power cliques have less leverage on the congregation. (2) When power cliques have formed, opening up and slowing down the decision making processes of the congregation create less pressure and, therefore, less opportunity for further polarization.

Out of balance: change can be a problem

Cliques are more apt to form during periods of major organizational problem solving. Any change in group life upsets the organization's equilibrium. Change creates uncertainty and sets off attempts to return to the status quo. Groups, therefore, contain a built-in tendency to resist change. When major changes or significant problems arise, a change-resistant clique may develop.

In order to guarantee predictability, groups structure their lives. For instance, a "pecking order" emerges to show who the group feels controls resources. The more perceived resources, the higher the status a group member is assigned. The difficulty with the natural group need for a measure of predictability arises when preserving the past against the present or the future becomes a fundamental subgroup agenda. Then change-resistant cliques take root.

Several steps can be taken to help groups manage uncertainty and solve problems. Slow paced and broad based decision making provides a beginning point for problem solving. Additionally, planned incremental change efforts ease organizational transitions.

Closed systems: the congregation as clique

Cliques are often observed in closed social systems. Group life revolves around two parts: an external system, like the denomination or the community surrounding a congregation, and an internal system, the congregation itself. The more insulated a church becomes, the less impact the external system has on the internal system. The more independently a church operates in its community, the more it tends to develop into a total congregational clique. Since churches, like all groups, tend to resist outside impacts, it's easy for congregations to consider their internal functioning to be their own business and no one else's. There's a built-in tendency for churches to close themselves and become cliquish.

Open church systems are sensitive to their communities and have permeable boundaries so people can move from the congregation to the community and back again. When the entire church becomes a closed clique, the congregation's ability to be "in the world" and to leaven, influence, and convert the world is limited. At its extreme the closed system prays,

Bless me and my wife,
My son John and his wife.
We four.
No more.

Sociologically, that perspective can be explained. Theologically, the church as a total clique is unthinkable.

Working with Congregational Cliques

Since cliques can't be ordered out of existence, the informal organization must be cared for. How?

Admit that cliques exist. Families, clubs, and churches have members who naturally share common interests and the strong emotions underlying those ties.

Sensitize leaders to the informal organization. Individual behavior becomes secondary to the clique's agenda. Cliques make conformists of their members.

Identify cliques in the congregation. Most of us are aware of the cliques we aren't part of. We often, however, are blind to the cliques we belong to. Our cliques are simply "our friends." Let me offer a broad catalog of common church cliques. Look for yourself in this listing as you identify possible cliques in your congregation.

The pastor and other ministers in the church provide an information and power center, which attracts people. Elected leaders, those who are assigned by the congregation to attend to the formal ministries, programs, and goals of the church, furnish another set of special interests for clique formation. One-issue members may feel drawn to either of these two cliques when interests coincide.

The informal leaders, who have influence but hold no elected position, are another group that attracts cliques.

These persons may not teach Sunday school classes or sing in the choir, but they have the clout to make direction setting either very easy (if they agree) or virtually impossible (if they disagree).

Active members, even if they are only "auditors" who attend worship and nothing else, can be stirred into some kind of emotional allegiance and drawn into a clique. Fringe members may join cliques as a way to get into the core of the congregation or as an avenue to power.

Work to align the formal and informal organizations of the congregation. Cliques ration warmth and acceptance. They hold the threat of "out" over their members who want to remain "in." Conformity is the price clique members pay for organizational and personal control. If the interests of cliques and the church's goals match up, the goals of the congregation will be met—and often exceeded.

VI

Crazymakers:
Sabotaging Communication

Some difficult church members attack with fixed bayonets. Others, however, slip behind the lines under cover of darkness and dynamite bridges. These sneakier ones are crazymakers.[1] They practice their passive-aggressive tactics quietly but effectively. The proof of their sabotage of communication is the utter confusion of those who try to converse with these crazymakers. The crazymaker keeps the upper hand.

Logic and Language No One Understands

We think or say, "You're making me crazy!" That's our response when our communication gets derailed by crazymakers. The logic or the language we encounter in the crazymaker throws us off-balance. We don't understand where their conversation is going.

Recently I saw the comedian George Burns being interviewed. He was asked what it was like to be on stage with his late wife Gracie Allen. He replied that their brand of "straight man and scatter brain" comedy was easy for him to do but tough for Gracie. George said he'd ask a simple question and Gracie would take off on five minutes of nonsense. In fact, one factor in Gracie's eventual retirement was the difficulty she had in memorizing page after page of unrelated, illogical nonsequiturs. For example, George would inquire about Gracie's brother and she'd make some rambling comment about the weather and then move on to mention two or three other completely irrelevant matters. There wasn't any connection between what she had just said or what she would say next. Gracie Allen was a comedic crazymaker.

Most crazymakers aren't so amusing. They're more like Lucy in the *Peanuts* comic strip who entices Charlie Brown to let her hold the football for his kick just one more time. He finally puts his trust in her, and she again moves the ball sending him cartwheeling through the air. The result of the crazymaker's work usually isn't funny and probably isn't constructive.

Sometimes the crazymaker's tool is language. Do you remember the special jargon Casey Stengel used to describe baseball? Sportswriters loved to interview Ol' Case because they could fill several columns trying to unravel and explain what he'd said. Stengel once explained, "Good pitching will beat good hitting every time—and vice versa." Huh? Stengel made sports fans a little crazy.

On other occasions crazymakers use warped logic. I heard a televised discussion on the Israel-Lebanese troop withdrawal pact. Two diplomats were proudly claiming that the document was written in such perfect diplomatic doubletalk that both sides can make it say what they want it to say. The results? The negotiations can go indefinitely! Somehow the logic of that process escapes me. We're left a bit crazy when no agreement is reached that really settles things. We're caught in the crazymaker's web and kept under his or her control. Cleaner communication would serve us better.

A Crazymaker Is . . .

How do crazymakers in a congregation behave? Think of the ways you'd complete the sentence, "A crazymaker is . . ." Do any of the following statements match your experiences with crazymakers?

A crazymaker is . . .

- Someone who makes a cutting remark and then claims, "I'm only kidding!"
- A person who introduces a subject and then refuses to discuss it.
- Someone who brings up a subject that doesn't fit any agenda.
- Someone who pulls the rug out from under you and then asks why you're sitting on the floor.
- A person who "goes by the book" even when the situation doesn't require it.
- Someone who explodes for no apparent reason.
- A person who claims "It doesn't matter" when it obviously does matter.
- A person who says sweetly, "I don't want to be picky, but . . ." and then proceeds to be picky and not sweet.
- A person who says yes but means no.
- Someone who keeps changing the subject.
- A person who accepts your gift and then criticizes it.
- Someone who can't make a decision.
- A person who's mad about one thing but flies off the handle about something else.
- Someone who orders you to do something "just because."
- A person who "doesn't care where we go" but refuses every suggestion you make.

- Someone who asks a question and then ignores your answer.
- Anyone who begins a conversation with "I wanted to tell you something of vital importance but I can't remember what it was."
- A person who keeps asking you questions but never shuts up so you can respond.
- Someone who makes a statement about themselves to you and adds "as if you care."
- A person who listens politely and then ignores your advice.
- Someone who asks for feedback and then takes offense at any remark you venture.

The Case of the Suicidal Crazymaker

It's unnerving to read a man's suicide note to him and have him pass it off casually as unimportant. Here's what happened.

Mary, our youth programs coordinator, was a single woman in her early twenties. One evening as she was taking several young people home after a youth activity, Mary handed the last boy to leave her car a sealed letter with instructions to read it later. The letter turned out to be a suicide note. After the boy read Mary's letter and consulted his parents, he called me. I immediately called Mary and tried to arrange a meeting with her. She resisted and only agreed to come to my office when she realized that I was going to come to her home. We sat down, and I tried to communicate my concern for her. Mary was very nonchalant about the situation. She insisted nothing was wrong with her. Finally, I read her letter aloud. Even then she claimed there was nothing for me to worry about.

Mary had very little to say. Her only overt concern was that her parents might learn about her suicide letter.

I tried to assure Mary of my care for her. I emphasized how highly the congregation valued her work. I prayed with her, but nothing seemed to reach her. Finally, I was able to get Mary to agree to get in touch with our city's suicide prevention service. In spite of all I tried to do, I spent an anxious night hoping Mary wouldn't harm herself. In this unusual circumstance, Mary became a crazymaker. She was simultaneously asking for and rejecting help. Like most crazymakers, Mary was sending contradictory communication signals.

What's That Saboteur's Name?

Crazymakers come in sundry varieties. Let me name some of the saboteurs. Have you had run-ins with any of these types?

The Double Binder. My phone rang at home one day. The distraught lady on the other end of the line identified herself and asked me if I would conduct her mother-in-law's funeral. I didn't recognize her name and inquired if she or her mother-in-law were members of my church. Neither of them were, she reported. She had picked me at random because my name was the most "religious" looking minister's name in the yellow pages! After I got over the shock of thinking of Dale as a hallowed name, I agreed to conduct their funeral. (I was touched by the fact that this family had no religious ties in our community. I hoped this ministry might open the door to reaching them.)

No sooner had I agreed to lead the funeral than she sprang the double bind. Her family wanted a nonreligious funeral!

How's that for a double bind? I went from the minister with the most religious name in the phone book to someone who might do a nonreligious funeral in about ten seconds! (Further conversation helped me discover that her definition of a "religious" funeral was a service with a long, long sermon. We were able to plan a brief service, and I established a long-term relationship with this family.) For a moment she made me crazy.

The Subject Changer. This crazymaker can't be kept on the subject. If the topic under discussion gets a little too close for his comfort, he simply shifts to a different issue. Listeners are thwarted because they thought they had a fix on the flow of the conversation, but then they don't.

The Blamesman. This crazymaker says or does something inappropriate and stirs the anger of his listener. When the listener's anger flares, the crazymaker responds with "just kidding, just kidding." The crazymaker then acts as if he has been unjustly attacked by the other over an insignificant incident.

The Short Fuse. Intimidation allows this crazymaker to control the communication agenda. The victim picks up the signals of unhappiness and tiptoes around emotionally in order to avoid upsetting the crazymaker.

The Overloader. When this crazymaker senses that an issue is about to be resolved and, therefore, his control may slip away, he simply throws out more ideas than can be processed. This usually bogs communication down and gives the crazymaker opportunity to drop the whole issue as too complex and beyond solving. The victim is left totally frustrated.

Communicating with the Crazymaker

How do you deal with a crazymaker? Nothing works automatically since this difficult person is so indirect with his aggression and you're the one who's left looking like the bad guy. However, try these hints.

- Name the game. Tell the crazymaker what's happening to you. Crazymaking is futile when exposed.
- Talk about the crazymaking process. Crazymakers will use all kinds of ploys to keep you from breaking their patterns.
- Enlist help. A church group can bring collective pressure to bear in an effort to develop healthier communication in the congregation.
- Keep the relationship highly structured.

Revelation: God's Side of Communication

Communication involves revealing information. In the Bible, revelation has a distinctly theological flavor and almost exclusively refers to God and divine activity. God takes initiative to reveal himself. We encounter him by waiting openly and hopefully. The Old Testament centers on God's liberation of Israel. So crucial is the Exodus experience to Israel's history that her faith consists basically of a rehearsal of the mighty acts of God.

The book of Revelation is personal and transactional. God enters into dialogue with persons; he calls and invites us into relationship with him. God approaches us in the personal, incarnational form of Christ to establish a personal covenant with each of us.

Jesus Christ is the definitive revelation of God. He makes the redemptive flow of history and the words of the prophets relative. Christ is the mediator and final expression of who God is for us. The Bible, the record of God's revelation to us, is interpreted by Christ, the living Word of God. The last word in communication, theologically speaking, is God in Christ for us.

VII

Sane Communication Among Sensitive Christians

There is no way *not* to communicate. Even the crazymaker communicates confusion. What's needed in the church is more sensitive and accurate communication. Since we've traditionally had more emphasis and better resources for speech and written communication, I've put more weight in this chapter on other dimensions of the communication process: metatalk, listening, and non-verbal clues.

Listening Between the Lines

Some words and phrases are clues to what we mean unconsciously in spite of what we say. For example, when I lead into a statement with "as you know," I'm about to speak down to you on the assumption that you really don't know or I wouldn't waste my time and yours with something we both understand. When a friend of mine introduces a statement with "clearly," I automatically brace myself. What that person is about to say probably won't be clear to either of us. Such clue words and phrases are termed "metatalk" and signal us to read between the lines of what's being said.[1] In fact, when I hear myself using metatalk, I check my logic or my motives. I may be trying too hard to convince myself or my listeners.

Let me alert you to some types of metatalk. "In my humble opinion" is a "halo hider" intended to mask false modesty. "Would you be kind enough to" is a "softener" angled toward influencing listeners positively. "What do you think about" is an "interester" designed to get involvement and agreement. "I know you don't want to discuss it" introduces a "downer" used to put hearers in a defensive posture. Well, you see how metatalk works. A knowledge of metatalk helps us listen more perceptively to our own conversation and the statements of others.

Ears to Hear

Poor listeners miss a lot. In round figures, the average person spends about 10 percent of his waking day writing, 15 percent reading, 30 percent talking, and 45 percent listening. (Students spend more like 60 percent of their days listening.) Poor listening habits penalize us severely.

Why aren't we able to listen better? We turn speakers off for a variety of reasons.

- Emotional factors—Stereotypes and personal insecurities hinder us from accurate hearing.
- Audio factors—Noise distractions, like background conversations or street sounds, affect our ability to take in information.
- Visual factors—Detracting mannerisms, such as yawning or clearing a desk, block good listening.
- Pace factors—We speak at a rate of about 120-155 words per minute. Our minds, however, can process 400 to 800 words each minute. The time gap between how fast we send information and how fast we receive information encourages us to "wool gather" and to fill our

minds with our own concerns. These random thoughts lessen our concentration on others' communications.

- Rebuttal factor—Most of us listen with some idea of countering the other's viewpoint. So we tune out and construct our own argument. The unfortunate result is simultaneous monologues, two folks who are talking without either of them listening.
- Advice-giving factors—Few of us enjoy or even use the advice others give us so freely. We prefer our own solutions and filter out advice (unless we're in a very dependent state of mind).

Listening is an underdeveloped skill. Most of us forget 75 percent of what we hear almost immediately. Therefore, three listening skills are crucial to sharpening our ability to hear sensitively. (1) Listening for facts calls for us to concentrate, pull out the major points of a presentation, repeat them to yourselves, and sum up. (2) Listening for feelings demands that we work to decode the emotional messages others are constantly sending. (3) Seeing what you hear or listening with your eyes forces us to take nonverbal communication seriously. In summary, we are poor listeners because it's such hard work. When we listen intently, our bodies respond with slight increases in blood pressure, heartbeat, and temperature. The cost of poor listening is so high that the payoff in improved communication makes the effort worthwhile.

Understanding Nonverbal Communication

Our culture is undergoing a slight but significant shift in communication style. We've long considered speech the primary mode humankind uses in communicating with each other. A growing interest in nonverbal communication is emerging, however. The nonlinguistic aspects of interpersonal communication include posture, tone of voice, facial expression, use of space, gestures, body movement, eye contact, vocal pauses, touch, and the impact of clothing styles.

Some resarchers claim as much as 90 percent of the impact of human communication is nonverbal. Their work points out several contrasts between verbal and nonverbal communication:

Verbal	*Nonverbal*
Conscious	Unconscious
High social value	Not recognized socially
Descriptive of emotion	Actual emotion
Rational	Subjective
Truth content can be manipulated	Truth content generally reliable

Some generalizations can be drawn from what we know about nonverbal communication:

- Nonverbal communication has a cultural and/or situational flavor. For example, many movements are random and vary in meaning from culture to culture. If we jump to conclusions and interpret behavior and motives every time someone blinks an eye or crosses a leg, we'll often be misled.
- Our bodies are generally disposed to convey the truer meanings of our expressions. Nonverbal clues are helpful supplements in communication.
- When our verbal and nonverbal messages conflict, the listener-observer invariably (and correctly) relies on our nonverbals.

- Healthy communication occurs when verbal statements and nonverbal behaviors coincide or are congruent.

Some common features of nonverbal communication can make church leaders more effective communicators. Several types of nonverbals are readily "readable."

It Goes with the Territory

Each of us has zones of territory we treat as our own personal space. The study of this phenomenon is called proxemics, or how we structure space unconsciously.

The way we behave in elevators is one interesting illustration of territoriality. Typically, if a person rides an elevator alone, he or she will stand in the middle of the car toward the rear of the space. If a second person comes into the elevator, both occupants tend to move into the back corners of the car. The next two riders take the front corners. The uncomfortable scramble begins when the fifth (and any additional) person comes aboard. Our problem is that we try to take up no space at all when we're crowded together with strangers on an elevator.

Proxemics has pointed out that we have a "bubble" of space around our bodies. That personal space extends about an arm's length in front of us, only a few inches from our sides, and four to six feet behind men and a little less for women. When someone invades our bubble uninvited and unwanted, we feel uneasy. We don't like to have others stand or sit too close to us. Some cultures allow for closer proximity, however, without discomfort. Church leaders need to take territory into account in arranging seating and in making work spaces comfortable.

Have you noticed how awkward a conversation feels in a crowded elevator? When people are bunched together in an elevator, the floor indicator light takes on a hypnotic attraction. Everyone stares at it silently, an unspoken element of elevator etiquette. There's a terrific pressure not to speak. A playful friend of mine decided to break the ice in a packed hospital elevator by mimicking a popular men's underwear commercial. "I feel good all under," he spoke into the silence. After a few seconds, a surly voice from the back of the car growled, "Buddy, if you say one more word, I'll stuff your shorts in your mouth!" Church leaders must become sensitive to proxemics; it goes with the territory.

The Eyes Have It

A friend of mine bet his wife he could guess a majority of the identities of the truthful contestants on the popular old television show, "To Tell the Truth." He turned off the sound and was able to predict the real contestants correctly over 70 percent of the time. My friend was so successful that the program invited him to appear and tell his secret. The key to his predictions? Reading nonverbals, especially eye movement. The phony contestants usually gave themselves away by the way they moved their eyes.

Eye management, termed oculesics, is an interesting branch of nonverbal communication. Each culture has its own rules for eye management. In American culture, we're taught not to stare. When approaching someone on the sidewalk, we "dim our lights" or glance away. We also know that staring at another person suggests we view him as a non-person. For example, when James Baldwin, the black novelist, became a major literary figure several years ago, he said he could always spot the racists at parties for authors: they looked right through him as if he were invisible.

Myths have grown up around the way we handle our gaze. The Mende, an African tribe, believe the dead can reappear in human form and can be readily recognized because they never look the living in the eye. Not surprisingly, the Mende are extremely wary of people who refuse to look at others during conversations.

The poet Magnus spoke of the "bewitching speech of the eyes." Probably he would have been fascinated by researchers' discoveries about eye management. Did you know that people look directly at each other about 60 percent of the time when they are talking? Did you know that people look at each other more while listening than while talking? Did you know that only about one-third of the time we spend looking at the persons we talk to is spent in direct eye contact or mutual gaze? Did you know that too much direct eye contact between persons of the same sex implies aggression (like a boxer's attempt to psych out his opponent by staring)? Did you know that staring between persons of the opposite sex has sexual overtones? Did you know that counselors often arrange their office chairs at slight angles so eye management is simplified? Did you know that some conjoint marriage therapists feel it's almost impossible for spouses with good relationships to lie to each other while looking directly into each other's eyes? Did you know that most of us can't blink and think at the same time? Did you know that when we're upset, we blink rapidly? Did you know that we also blink at the end of sentences and when we finish a thought? Oculesics provides important clues for those of us in ministry.

Bodies Talk

Our bodies "speak" a language called kinesics. The meanings of a number of bodily movements are considered virtually universal. The vertical head nod, for instance, is almost universally recognized as a "yes" sign. This movement has been observed in primitive cultures and even among persons born deaf and blind. By the same token, the horizontal head shake is almost always a negative sign. Hand waves have been observed for thousands of years as a sign of beginning or ending an encounter. Tilting the head slightly to the side denotes attentiveness, even in animals like dogs.

Kinesics are observed in all types of social settings. When we pledge oaths of honesty, we place hands over our hearts, a gesture of sincerity. In business situations, my father claims he was never able to sell anyone an insurance policy who had his arms folded across his chest, a sign of closedness or defensiveness. Labor negotiators note that an unbuttoned coat is often a clue of openness and of an increased chance of concluding the bargaining process.

The Nonverbals of Living Space

Places, like persons, have nonverbals. Remember the original Archie Bunker television show? There was a "sacred" space in Archie and Edith's living room—Archie's chair! Anyone who sat in Archie's special chair created a crisis. Only Archie was allowed to sit there. (That chair became so well-known that it now is on display in the Smithsonian Institution.) Our homes have their special spaces—pieces of furniture, favorite rooms, a place at the meal table we think of as "mine" in a personal sense.

Even colors have impact. A friend of mine pastored a church whose worship space was decorated in earth tones—warm golds and browns. He found preaching in that space comfortable and relaxing. Then he moved to a new congregation whose sanctuary was trimmed with a pale blue and stark white color scheme. Although the congregation was made up of exciting, well educated, attentive folks, my friend found preaching in that space was a labor. Why? He decided the primary communication barrier was the setting itself. In fact, he felt the color scheme was a basic problem. According to my friend, the nonverbals of the worship space dampened the communication climate in the second building.

Color schemes and lighting set moods. We've known that for a long time. But some colors seem to have strange effects on us. Reds have been found to increase appetite and the rate at which one eats. Studies also reveal that red seems to make table turning in restaurants more frequent.

This science is called chromotherapy and has had its most dramatic use in the control of violent criminals and mental patients. Passive pink, a bubble gum color, has been found to have a pacifying or calming effect. Roughly fifteen hundred hospitals and correctional institutions now use pink rooms to relax unmanageable persons. A few enterprising coaches have had the opposing team's dressing room painted pink to create a "down" atmosphere!

A home visit is a revealing event for any person who's trying to minister. Note the sacred places. "Read" what furnishings, decorations, and clutter can tell you about the inhabitants of a living or work space. Communication is all around us.

VIII

Hostility:
Hot Heads Instead of Warm Hearts

Recently a young minister friend told me that the biggest surprise and disappointment during his first two years out of seminary had been encountering a hostile church member. "For the first time in my ministry," he said, "I've discovered not everybody likes me. Even though I've tried to talk with this man about our relationship, he denies there's any problem at all and refuses to discuss my discomfort. Then I discover that he's continuing to criticize all I try to do. I don't know how to deal with hostility!"

Hostile persons are difficult to deal with. (Let me distinguish between anger, a legitimate emotion stirred by an actual grievance, and hostility, injurious feelings intended to hurt.) Hostile actions range from edginess and complaining to physical and emotional assault. What explains the perpetually hostile church member?

How the Behavioral Sciences Explain Hostility

All kinds of psychological and medical reasons have been given for hostile behavior.[1] Do any of these ideas ring true in your experience?

Some theorists note that the fight-flight pattern fits lots of conflict situations. Like the caveman who occasionally found himself face-to-face with a saber-toothed tiger in some jungle clearing, we too prefer to flee and avoid conflict when possible. But if we're cornered, we'll fight.

The survival of the fittest is an old explanation of aggression. Darwin claimed that violence served a useful purpose—it eliminated the weaker creatures. By the turn of the twentieth century, social Darwinism endorsed monopolies in business and territorial acquisition. In that spirit, Teddy Roosevelt described the Spanish-American War as "a moral tonic."

Animal studies have noted that wild beasts instinctively fight over territory, status, and mates. That sounds like humans as far as it goes. That is, we have conflict over those things too. But humans also fight over values like religion and politics.

Mark Twain, in one of his typical tall tales, tells how concerned he became over the discord among God's creatures. He decided to take matters in hand.

Twain claimed he built a cage and put a dog and a cat in it. After a period of training, the dog and cat learned to live peaceably together. Then he added a pig, a goat, a kangaroo, some birds, and a monkey. After a few adjustments, they too learned to live in harmony. Twain became so encouraged with his successes that he added an Irish Catholic, a Presbyterian, a Jew, a Muslim from Turkestan, and a Buddhist from China, along with a Baptist missionary captured on the China trip. In a very short time there wasn't a single living thing left in the cage! Twain was right even with his exaggerations. We humans fight over everything animals do—and more!

Freud attempted the first systematic explanation of hostile behavior. He described a "life force" in his early writings. When World War I made him account for the hostile impulses in humankind, Freud then proposed a "death wish." When "thanatos," as he called it, was turned inward, people became cruel, depressed, and suicidal. When turned outward, persons became hostile and warlike.

Hostility's Cultural Face

Our Western Hemisphere is the world's most violent culture. Handguns, for instance, are more prevalent in the United States than in any other country—about 135 million or roughly two per household. Over twenty-thousand Americans are shot and die as a result each year.

Our television programming portrays violence as commonplace too. Children's cartoons average eight episodes of violence per hour. By age eighteen the average American youngster will have viewed more than eighteen thousand murders on television. No wonder an American social activist claimed that "violence is as American as apple pie."

The pervasiveness of hostile activity has made us a calloused nation. A man was struck by a car in a busy Nashville intersection during the rush hour. Drivers simply steered around him for twenty minutes before someone finally assisted him. Some of those who ignored the man's plight later said they assumed someone else would help the injured man. Montana has even passed a "good Samaritan" law to require motorists to aid each other in areas where assistance may be many miles away.

Christians Fuss Too

What accounts for church fights? Like others we Christians disagree over differences—different goals, different beliefs, different information. We also fall into conflict over similarities. There may only be one leader position available and several "volunteers" are willing to be "selected" to serve. Additionally, Christian theology is plainspoken about sin—our general human cussedness. Jung termed sin as our "God-almighty complex." We typically want the supreme, controlling position in human affairs. That tendency obviously places us in conflict with each other.

Hostility Is . . .

What do you feel when you're hostile? Relate these statements to the hostile church members you know.
- Bottled-up fear.
- Feeling forced into someone else's mold.
- Being tailgated by a tractor trailer truck.
- Wanting to tell the boss off but not having the guts to do it.
- An aggressive reaction to frustration.
- A highly charged emotional state.
- Not having an opportunity to speak your mind.
- An emotional release of aggression.
- Cutting comments with humorous overtones.
- Feeling put down for your values and beliefs.
- Neither communication nor confrontation when both are needed.
- Having a disagreement immediately before a worship service.
- The negative expression of anger toward others or myself.

Why Complain?

Complainers in the church are low-octane hostiles. Why complain? Basically, they feel helpless and not in control of their life situation. So they "share their misery" with whomever is handy. Never satisfied, the complainer uses whining as his primary way of relating to others.

What do complainers expect? They expect their grievances to be made right. They don't want doubletalk or to be ignored; they want their problems solved now. Assurance of prompt action is crucial to the complainer. Additionally, they want to get their gripes off their chests. They expect to be able to express their dissatisfaction and frustration. An understanding hearing is important to complainers. Furthermore, some complainers gripe just for fun. They can be disarmed a bit by a friendly smile and a quick greeting. This type isn't looking for solutions or sympathy. They want to project blame on others for their problems. Finally, complainers make you feel you aren't doing enough for them. The result is that the complainer is in control and you feel guilty.

Complaining isn't pleasant for leaders to hear. Does griping serve any purpose for the complainer? It does give a release for anger. And, complaining lends a measure of self-control when the circumstances really can't be changed. Leaders need to remember that complainers are rarely leaders themselves. We are where they want to be.

How do you cope with a complainer? (1) Don't reinforce the complaining. Don't argue with a complainer. If you do, you're playing his game. (2) Deflect complaints. Your resident complainer gripes, "That choir anthem stunk!" Try a response like "Really? I like that style of music occasionally." Keep the complainer out of the spotlight.

The Case of the Hostile Letter

No one likes to receive hostility—particularly a letter. (The only thing worse than a hostile letter is an *anonymous* hostile letter.) My hateful letter was signed by an ordinary-looking, thirtyish, single man named Louis. I was startled by the tone of Louis' letter since I'd only been his pastor for a few months and had had only casual contacts with him. But, I had noticed an atmosphere of coldness between us. I didn't realize that his silence masked his hostility toward me.

Louis' gripe? I was too happy. Nobody's life could go as pleasantly as he thought mine was going. Louis' complaint was a new one to me. Too happy? His letter threw me off stride. What had I done? What could I do? I knew I had tried to establish a relationship with him. And I knew I would see him around church all the time. I also discovered that his hostility toward me was not an isolated event. Louis was our congregation's resident hostile!

I called Louis and, in spite of a hostile reception, was able to make an appointment to visit with him the next day. Talking with Louis was tough work. He was angry because I acted happy and he wasn't happy at all. Further conversation helped me discover that Louis and I had a number of similar experiences in our backgrounds. When I told Louis some of the painful events in my life, he was just as perplexed as I had been by his letter. I shared with him the difference Christ had made in my life. That broke the dam. Louis began talking about how unsure he was about whether Christ really loved him.

Our relationship began to mellow and grow. Louis and I had found some common ground. No longer was he so angry at my joy in life; no longer was I as intimidated by his hostility. Although Louis didn't stop being our church hostile, I had established a non-defensive basis for working with Louis without fighting.

My experience with Louis reminds me of some advice an army book gives to noncommissioned officers. The book tells how to make men who have quarreled become friends again. The men are assigned to wash the same window— one on the inside, the other on the outside. This forces them to look at each other for a period of time. Invariably they begin to laugh and the tension between them dissolves. A common experience often provides a setting where relationships can start over again.

Hostility's Fallout

There's a hostile church member type who's even more difficult to deal with than either a privately hostile Louis or a chronic complainer. Who? The openly conspicuous (even satisfied) hostile!

Consider your church's resident hothead. What's the payoff for dumping hostility onto the congregation? First, there's veto power. A person who's willing to make a public scene is often given extra space by the group. That latitude can be translated into power—power to block ministries, decisions, and programs. Second, the overtly hostile member can ultimately hijack a congregation's mission. By intimidating a group completely, the hostile can cause a church to adjust its purpose. At his worst a hostile's angry threats can even prompt an abandonment of the congregation's vision of its ministry.

How can a church be so thoroughly intimidated by a hostile member? Generally, congregations image themselves as basically nice groups. So, they can be stymied by members who are willing to be "bad." The congregation's uncertainty gives hostiles lots of leverage and sometimes complete control. Beneath this outcome is the assumption that Christians don't have conflicts. That isn't the case. Christians confront lovingly in order to advance God's kingdom. That quality of confrontation begins in local churches.

Healthy congregations can't choose their members. So they must at least tolerate their hostiles. Better yet, they can show their hostiles that they will not be railroaded by threats. One fact is clear. A healthy congregation can't allow one or two negative members to select or change the church's mission. Hopefully, a firm stance can begin a reconciling process.

Reconciliation: God's Activity

Reconciliation is the New Testament's word for the changed relationship between God and man made possible by the death and Resurrection of Jesus Christ. Based on a noun and two verbs found about a dozen times in the writings of Paul, reconciliation is the distinctive activity of God. Radical changes in a person's life result from God's reconciling work in history through Christ. Hostility and estrangement are put away in Christ.

An important distinction needs to be made for the benefit of those of us who want to help broken relationships be restored. Reconciliation, making friends out of enemies, is God's exclusive work; conflict management is a ministry open to all Christian peacemakers. Reconciliation is an act already accomplished; conflict management is a process to be designed for congregations' special needs. Jesus Christ has provided reconciliation. Christians can't replace Jesus. We do not have the resources or the responsibility to reconcile enemies or factions. No matter how concerned we become for the fragmented relationships of fellow Christians or congregations, we can't reconcile others. That's God's arena and his gift to us. It's a good gift!

IX

The Church Faces Conflict

What happens when hostility overflows into the congregation? Let's look at several dimensions of conflict.

The Three-Cornered Ring

Most social conflict is triangular—a "for" position, an "against" position, and a neutral position. That is, when you and I disagree strongly about any issue, we deadlock and instinctively seek an ally. We know intuitively that two against one creates favorable odds. The conflicts in congregations are, therefore, often fought in this three-cornered ring.

This odd-man-out tactic is not very constructive for close-knit groups like churches and families for one simple reason: triangles aren't win-win strategies. In a triangle someone is, by definition, defeated, squeezed out, and made into a loser. When any member of a congregation is humiliated, the entire family of faith loses because the morale of the church is undermined. Healthy congregations work to find and implement win-win resolutions to conflicts.

I've noticed that nearly all of the requests for advice in the Dear Abby and Ann Landers columns are stalemates. The advice-giver is, then, invited (or enticed) into the deadlock. Abby and Ann stay out of these triangles as much as possible. When they choose to enmesh themselves in others' conflicts, they are prepared to forfeit their relationship (if any) to the persons they ally against. Their behavior speaks volumes to church leaders. We must count the cost carefully before we step into the third corner of others' conflicts.

Who Owns the Problem?

Who owns the problem when there's conflict within the congregation? The person who's upset. But in congregational conflict situations, it's tough to leave the problem with its "owner." For example, many ministers are natural rescuers. When people bring their problems to the minister, they may be looking for a way to "get the monkey off their backs." Rescuers, ministers or laypersons, often end up with a backfull of monkeys. In conflict management a good guideline is to make sure the same person who brought in the monkey leaves with him too!

Monkey watching is crucial for a reason more important than self-protection. Problems solved by non-owners rarely stay solved—unless ownership of the solution is taken. If I solve your problems and make your decisions, then I'm responsible when my solutions to your problems don't work out right.

In a larger context, when does conflict in the church become a congregation-wide issue? When the problem changes the climate and atmosphere of the church, then the congregation at large must come to grips with a conflict process. The monkey is on everyone's back then.

Types of Church Conflicts

Generally speaking, when congregations fight, two issues are in the foreground—facts and feelings. That is, some conflicts are triggered by issues of substance, matters of fact, and their interpretation. Other disagreements are basically emotional personality conflicts.

Social scientists, for example, have discovered that riots in the American culture can be classified into two categories: instrumental and expressive. Instrumental riots occur when groups resort to violence because of discontent over specific, substantive issues. Most riots are of this type and happen when real grievances haven't been heard or addressed. Labor, prison, and anti-war riots usually fall into this classification.

Expressive riots erupt when many people in a minority group use violence to show dissatisfaction with conditions. These uprisings are symbolic gestures of widespread discontent. These expressive riots have occurred mostly since 1960 and have often involved the effects of racial discrimination, such as prejudice in schools, jobs, and housing. While growing out of facts, the primary stimulus for expressive riots is emotional outlet.

Factual conflicts call for mediation. Feelings require ventilation. Some congregations handle one type of conflict better than the other.

Congregational Conflict Styles

Do you know your congregation's conflict management style? I've discovered three primary approaches churches use to deal with hostility. The "pleaser" style is most common. This approach majors on cooperation and minors on assertiveness. It's easy to see that a totally hostile member may intimidate a church of pleasers into accepting his solution whether they like his answer or not. It's also easy to see why this church develops the pattern of putting "them" before "me" or "us."

The second most used style is the "partner" approach. This style tries to balance out varying levels of cooperation and assertiveness. The result is a congregational "us" pattern, searching for a middle ground solution.

The pattern ranking a distant third is the "pusher" style. Pushers tend to be more assertive than cooperative. This style yields a "me" pattern of placing individual concerns above congregational ones.

Two sources of research have led me to these conclusions about congregational conflict coping styles. For several years I've used the Hostility Inventory to help a few hundred churchpeople clarify how they are affected by hostility and how they deal with it. I've noticed several emerging trends: (1) Religious people tend to be more positive and optimistic than the general population. Those of us in the church score low on the issues of negativism, resentment, and suspicion. (2) Christians are more indirect than direct in expressing hostility. We're fairly low in showing verbal hostility and assault. (3) Generally speaking, church men are more given to assault as an expression of hostility than women; church women are more apt to use verbal hostility than men. In summary, church folks seem to express their hostility in passive-aggressive, or "nicer," more indirect manners.

I've also used the Thomas-Kilmann Conflict Mode Instrument with church leaders in evaluating their behaviors in situations where interpersonal concerns aren't compatible. This instrument explores how we may respond to conflict with either cooperative or assertive actions (or some combination of the two). Five styles are identified by a division of thirty points. The most common styles of the two hundred or so persons in my sample are: compromising (7.43 points on the average); avoiding (7.11); accommodating (6.50); collaborating (5.94); and competing (3.13). These numbers suggest that church-people in conflict situations will first compromise. If that strategy doesn't work, then they will avoid the differences. As a third resort, they will then try to reach an accommodation. Assuming that step doesn't resolve the conflicts either, they attempt to collaborate. As a last resort, they will try to resolve their differences by competing in win-lose fashion.

There are pros and cons in the congregational styles mentioned above. What are the advantages?

- They fit volunteer organizations generally.
- They are sensitive to human relations.
- They lend themselves to congregational participation.
- They are fairly optimistic in relation to human nature.

Are there some disadvantages to the styles mentioned above? Yes, there are several.

- They tilt toward the status quo.
- They may set church leaders up as victims in conflict situations. That is, the over-cooperative styles use pleasers as doormats.
- They can invite underhanded pressure tactics if people naively assume every difference will automatically work out well "because this is the church."

Uses of Conflict in Congregations

Why do church members fight with each other? There are probably as many reasons as there are difficult church members. Four uses of conflict in congregations are, however, basic to exploring why difficulties arise in church groups. Note that two of the uses of conflict produce win-lose resolutions and the other two are win-win possibilities. Let's consider these conflict motivations on a spectrum from potentially most destructive to church health to most constructive.

The *power grab* is the most blatant use of conflict in the church. *Control* is the primary motive behind this win-lose strategy. In their less obvious forms, power grabs attempt to veto others' wishes by inhibiting, blocking, or even intimidating them. In its more overt arrangements, a power grab often involves forming open alliances. These coalitions usually cause polarities to be drawn (or overdrawn), creating an "us" versus "them" atmosphere. When a power grab is attempted, the congregation becomes politicized. "Going for the jugular" can divide congregations in ways that make healing of the breaches almost impossible.

Scapegoating, or diverting other frustrations onto the congregation, may also serve as a dubious use of conflict in churches. Job pressures, home and family demands, or even national concerns may get dumped on the church. Tragically, scapegoating happens in most cultures, including the United States. For example, in the American South when cotton prices dropped during the late nineteenth and early twentieth centuries, lynchings rose dramatically. When the economy soured, scapegoats were identified and frustrations from other sources were heaped on the blamed persons. *Blaming* is the basic motivation behind this win-lose style of fighting.

Taking *ownership of individual values* provides another use of congregational conflict. Value-rich areas of our lives—religion, family, money, sex, politics—provide arenas for exploring our personal commitments. Conflicts over these types of issues give us a chance to clarify, invest in, and take ownership of our deeper values. Conflicts that yield a cleaner ownership of our values can be win-win resolutions and are potentially healthy when two big "ifs" are present. "If" the processes for discussion and decision making are open and the structures are stable so the issues can be dealt with fairly. "If" church members can move from the narrow beginning of individual convictions to the broader concern of congregational beliefs. Personal *convictions* are the motivation for this conflict use.

Debating *basic mission issues* is still another use of church conflict. The process of building a congregational consensus is empowering for participants. Taking diversity seriously, hearing what fellow members are for (not just what they are against), exploring differences, defining and unfreezing polarities, and searching for the common ground of agreement help the church's basic purposes and goals develop. This process can become a unifying event for a church and offer win-win possibilities. *Consensus* provides the motivational background for this style of congregational conflict.

A special instance of conflict management occurs when a church leader is faced with confronting another member. A non-church case may illustrate this situation.

A Chewing Out from the View of the Chewee

He stood round shouldered and dejected. "What's the matter, Marty?" "Tomorrow's going to be a rough day," he answered. "How so?" I inquired. "I have to chew someone out." How rough can that be, I wondered silently. After all, Marty was the president of a major corporation. Power brokers asked his advice daily. His penthouse office was the length of a bowling alley, with carpet so deep I felt as if I was walking over a sand dune every time I visited Marty at work. Chewing someone out should be a simple matter for a man with Marty's authority.

"Well," I offered with all the confidence of a person who didn't know what he was talking about, "just march down to his office the first thing tomorrow morning and tell him to shape up!" A slow smile crept across Marty's face. "That isn't the way to chew someone out," he reacted. I was fascinated. "Tell me how to chew out an employee," I asked. Marty straightened and quietly taught me a lesson I've never forgotten.

"The first thing you do is call him into your office," Marty said. "Then you invite him to sit down. Next, you get up, come around the desk, and stand over him. You tell him in direct terms what you have to say. You don't even have to raise your voice."

When I thought of the nonverbals involved, I could see why Marty's approach was a high impact style. First, Marty got his supervisee onto his territory, his "turf." Second, he stood above his employee and created an over-under dynamic of literally talking down to the other person spatially. Third, he talked straight, without emotional and accusing language.

But, Marty was concerned about his suprvisee's feelings. Marty agreed with Frank A. Clark's philosophy: "Criticism, like rain, should be gentle enough to nourish a man's growth, without destroying his roots." (I didn't ask him, but I imagine that Marty was also careful not to convey the three universal nonverbal signs of hostility—snarling lips, glowering eyes, and knitted brows.) I was impressed that Marty confronted his employees with genuine concern. When he chewed someone out, he took the feelings of the "chewee" into account too.

Confrontation is usually uncomfortable. Do a motive and attitude check before you face another person about your differences.

X

Apathy: Letting St. George Do It

"A yawn is at least an honest opinion," so the saying goes. In most congregations, apathetic church members are prime candidates for yawning. They let George (or St. George) do it.

Routes to Apathy

Different roads lead to apathy. Limited opportunities, health difficulties, and disappointment create apathy in a few church members. Some take the weariness route of long service and eventual stagnation. Others follow the road of being unable to break into their church's core and lose their initial enthusiasm. The cost of this apathy is monumental. Southern Baptists have discovered, for instance, that slightly over one-fourth of their total denominational membership is inactive. While not an unusual statistic for large denominations, the loss of human resources because of apathy is staggering.

Some persons become apathetic because they burn out. These are the ones who are apt to be long-term church members who can't carry their heavy responsibilities any longer. Burned out leaders are depleted idealists, persons who tend to be over committed and under encouraged. Their weariness pushes them to give up and drop out. In the wise words of Vince Lombardi, the late coach of professional football's Green Bay Packers, "Fatigue makes cowards of us all."

Another category of church members who become apathetic is the unassimilated. Often newer congregation members, these persons can't get into meaningful service or into groups they view as attractive. Since they're shut out of their congregation's inner sanctums, they fall by the wayside.

One Explanation

John Savage has provided the Christian community with a helpful explanation of the apathetic and bored church member in his "anxiety-anger" complex.[1] Here's a shorthand version of Savage's research.

Savage notes that an anxiety-provoking event usually triggers the demotivation process. By anxiety, Savage means "the loss of a comfortable state, a feeling of being knocked off your equilibrium."

Cries for help follow. The upset church members signal, usually verbally, others in the congregation that they've been thrown off-balance. If the congregation ignores their cries, the lack of response deepens their anger.

This anger is described as feelings of displeasure, uneasiness, and resentment. Importantly, this anger is nearly always object oriented. So the natural response is to strike out in an attempt to get rid of the situations or objects producing the anger and anxiety.

Anger in the church may be focused in two directions. If the anger is turned toward others or toward the institution, it is expressed in resistance and/or rebellion. If this anger is turned inward on yourself, blame or guilt results.

What happens if these feelings of anger aren't resolved? In cases where the anger is directed outwardly, the church member may conclude there isn't any help outside himself. The resulting helplessness leads to apathy. When the anger, on the other hand, is inner-directed, the angry member decides there's no help inside himself. Hopelessness results, and the member experiences boredom. The primary outcome is less church activity, a survival tactic when everything else seems lost. They feel grief, give up, and drop out. Demotivation has taken root.

One of the most provocative findings in Savage's research is a six to eight-week "window of waiting." It is a time in limbo when the dropped-out church member gives the congregation a chance to recover him. If the church doesn't reach out to the dropout, he reinvests his time and re-engages his energy in family or non-church volunteer activity. His life stabilizes around his new interests, and the dropout is then doubly difficult to recover for productive church service.

Three significant opportunities for congregations to cope with apathy in their members are spotlighted in Savage's research. The cry for help, the time when anger is turned in or out, and while the dropout is living in limbo each offers chances for congregations to take positive initiative and show their care and concern for their apathetic members.

The Case of the Apathetic Deacon

My apathetic church member was elected to a key lay leadership role several years ago. However, he rarely attends church presently. He isn't mad at anyone. In discussions he shows lots of genuine concern for others and the church. But he isn't sufficiently motivated to act on his concern.

He used to be a drug addict. With treatment he broke his drug habit, got into the church, and became a workaholic all in one swoop. My apathetic member holds down a (more than full-time) supervisory job in a factory and farms six hundred acres in his "spare time." Consequently, he attends church only three or four times a year because he also volunteers to work on Sundays at his plant. No wonder home visits yield the "I'm too tired" excuses to invitations to get involved in church again.

The only energy my apathetic church member invests in his congregation is in an occasional short-term project—usually building and grounds improvement. In these projects he's highly efficient. Then he disappears again from the church for several months.

Can this apathetic member be involved again?

Apathy Is . . .

Describe apathy. Do these ideas ring true for you?

Apathy is . . .

- The feeling of floating.
- Complacency.
- Being overwhelmed and undervalued.
- Having no way out.
- Friday afternoon.
- A minister who has given up and given in.
- Not having anything to say about what's being done in your own church.
- A means of survival.

- Not caring whether you live or die.
- Monday morning after you've preached two sermons the day before and realize you've got to prepare two more for next Sunday.
- Not giving a hoot.
- Being content with things as they are.
- Not being all you can be.
- Having no goals.
- No feeling—that's the word's literal meaning in the Greek language.
- Inertia produced by feeling numbed by a problem, whether yours or someone else's.
- Letting George do it.
- A burned-out layperson.
- The reaction of any congregation when the sermon lasts past noon.
- Less than being alive.
- Emptiness.
- Having nowhere to go and no desire to get there.
- Feeling the church will do well enough financially without your offering.
- Deciding you can't make a difference by yourself.
- Having to help those who don't want any help.
- What you get when you don't involve others in church planning.
- A poor excuse for not doing anything.
- Saying, I've already done my part.
- A lack of concern or care for someone or something.
- Loneliness.
- Seeing the church as a spectator sport.
- Complaining about situations and then not doing anything to make those situations better.
- Actively looking for a free ride.

So You Never Made Who's Who?

Let's take a look at the lighter side of demotivation. Do you dial "0" and, instead of hearing the operator you're startled by "Your number can't be reached as dialed . . ."?

Is your photograph in your high school yearbook a gray square because you missed picture day . . . and no one besides you has noticed?

When you last interviewed for a job, did the interviewer ask you to list the schools you'd dropped out of?

Does your mother sometimes have difficulty remembering your name?

Did the publishers of Who's Who in America pass over you again this year?

If these questions strike a responsive chord in you, you're a likely candidate for a new organization, Who's Nobody in America. Two San Diego writers have calculated that roughly 220 million Americans will never be invited to be listed in Who's Who. So, they've begun the Who's Nobody volume published by (what else?) Nobody Press.[2]

By the way, overnight wonders need not apply. Three or four years of steady nobodiness is required. Who belongs so far? A woman who gave an intimate dinner party and was asked by several guests if she could point out the hostess since they wanted to leave and needed to thank her. A man with a 9:00 A.M. doctor's appointment who sat in the waiting room all day before the nurse finally asked him what he wanted. A lady from New Orleans who sent in a Polaroid snapshot with a white blob where her head should have been. An entire Newport, Kentucky, American Legion Post.

Who's Nobody may tickle your funny bone or strike a dagger into your feelings of insignificance. This organization reminds us that many people consider themselves nobodies. What more crucial group than a congregation to leaven a community by believing in its members? What more basic theological truth than reminding ourselves and others that they're created in the image of God and redeemed by the death and Resurrection of Jesus Christ? Motivation remains a fundamental issue in all of us. Some leaders, therefore, are willing to manipulate others in order to see action.

Watch for the Manipulator!

Who is the predominant personality of our age? According to Richard Restak, it's the manipulator, and he's everywhere.[3] He's a backslapper and a sweet-talker. He's a winner (at least on the outside). He has one standard of measurement for others: what can you do for me today? To get you to do what he wants, he has mastered the casual, quick, surface deal; the shallow, slick relationship is the manipulator's stock-in-trade.

Restak thinks the manipulator reduces every encounter to a win-lose contest and plays his slick and superficial role constantly. Because he lacks a sense of real identity, he uses his material and professional achievements as his proof that his style works.

Whether Restak is correct or not about how common the manipulator is, when we find one in the church, we're disappointed. The manipulator demotivates other members by undermining their ability to serve freely and fully. No one likes to be manipulated. Even more important is the risk that volunteers won't stand for manipulation; they simply drop out rather than work with a manipulating leader. A theological distinction can be made at this point. The manipulator forces from the outside. Our Lord urges us toward service from within.

Who Motivates the Christian?

Since motivation is generally considered an internal condition, the Holy Spirit is a primary source of motivation for the Christian. Three basic affirmations note the relationship between the Holy Spirit and the believer's motivation.

- The Holy Spirit dwells within the Christian. The Fourth Gospel describes the Holy Spirit as our counselor, the Spirit of truth, who dwells with us and will be in us (John 14:17).
- The Holy Spirit energizes the Christian. The Spirit provides us an internal support system and empowers us for service. Jesus promised us that he wouldn't leave us orphaned (John 14:18) and that he will be with us until the end (Matthew 28:20).
- The Holy Spirit is a primary "need-meeting" resource for the Christian. Christ's spirit ministers actively in us (John 14:25-31). That's a motivational reminder!

XI

Coping with Inertia

Apathetic congregations are bogged down, inert. They're turned inward on themselves but don't even serve their own concerns well. How can church leaders cope with congregational inertia?

The Sign of the Shrugged Shoulders

Some observers see our era rather negatively. They see our heroes as being unworthy of their status because of their idleness. Most of them seem to do little or nothing to attain that level. Shrugged shoulders and a "who cares" attitude symbolize our time in history. Our sin is apathy, not pride.[1] We leave our life's decisions to the snake, just like Adam and Eve did. We haven't been responsible stewards of our opportunities. We have sinned by omission. We have become less than our Creator has offered us. We have options and choices—but we don't select, elect, or shape our destinies. We don't care. We're looking for a way out. Passivity is our life-style. Does this overview describe the unmotivated church member?

The unmotivated church member is a powerless person. Christians are called to service, faith, risk, creativity, and leadership. But a lack of motivation undercuts our willingness to serve Christ and causes us to shrug our shoulders callously.

The Essential Difference

Recently I had an enlightening conversation with a friend who was a national sales manager for a major corporation before he entered the ministry. Previously, my friend had supervised a huge sales force. Now he pastors a sizable church and leads a large staff of laypersons in the ministry of his congregation. We were talking about the essential differences between corporate life and the church. The discussion shifted to the contrasts between motivating employees and church volunteers.

"What's the difference between motivating salesmen and Sunday school teachers?" I inquired. After a moment's thought, he answered, "You can't fire volunteers!" He's right. When employees aren't motivated to work, they can be fired. But volunteers serve out of a different set of motives. And church leaders are compelled by a covenant of concern to motivate volunteers, using "purer" approaches. After all, you can't fire your volunteers!

Testing the Motivational Climate

Church leaders are responsible for building a motivational climate in the congregation. Can you answer these questions about the motivational quotient of your church?

Does your church have a team spirit?

A "we" atmosphere is an important motivational feature in a healthy congregation. It's important that each of us feels that we're not the only person carrying the load. Have you heard about the farmer's method for motivating his mule? Periodically the farmer would call out: "Gittup, Blackie! Gittup, Spot! Gittup, Old Joe!"

A neighbor heard this exchange several times and finally couldn't contain his curiosity any longer. "How many names does that mule have?"

"Only one," the farmer replied. "His name is Young Joe. But he doesn't know his own strength. So I put blinkers on him, shout out three other names, and he thinks he's part of a hitch of four!"

It helps when others are helping us.

Where are the energy reservoirs in your congregation?

Most congregations have at least a few pockets of enthusiasm for specific ministries or projects. Folks can become almost fanatical about their favorite church interests—choir, Sunday school, or the church building. These energy reservoirs provide both a clue to and a resource for motivation.

Occasionally the church drains its energy reservoirs, either accidentally or deliberately. For instance, a new convert pressed his pastor for a ministry he could do. The pastor hesitated, because this new member was uneducated and crude. But the new Christian was persistent. Finally, to rid himself of the enthusiastic convert, the pastor gave him a supply of church letterhead stationery and the names of several other members who were behind in their gifts to the church.

A few days later the pastor received a letter from a prominent physician in the church.

Dear Pastor:
Enclosed is my check. This gift catches me up on my delinquent tithe.

Furthermore, I apologize that my attendance has been irregular lately. You can count on me to be in church every Sunday hereafter.

Please do me one favor. Tell your assistant that "dirty" is spelled with only one *T*, and skunk begins with *S*, not *C!*

Energy, while it needs the channeling church leaders can provide, is too rare to be squandered. Use the energy reservoirs to advance the congregation's ministry.

How do you pay your volunteers?

Employees are paid in wages, fringe benefits, and bonuses. Volunteers, on the other hand, are compensated through real, though intangible, payoffs. Employees are paid after the work is done from a checking account. Volunteers, however, are paid before the work is done out of a psychological savings account.

Volunteers operate out of more altruistic motives generally. Growth in others and yourself, service, and recognition are some psychological wages volunteers receive. For this reason, a high stroke atmosphere of appreciation and recognition nurtures the morale level of local congregations.

One retired pastor learned the importance of paying volunteers, but it was too late then. After retirement he was asked what he would do differently if he had his ministry to do over. "I'd preach more encouragement to my people," he answered. Stated otherwise, he would have paid his volunteers better. Motivation is serious business. But, just to change pace, let's look at motivation lightheartedly.

Sure-Fire Demotivators

Self-starters can be stymied. Enthusiasm can be dampened. You can learn to demotivate others (although I can't even guess why you'd deliberately want to know this "trick")! Yes, you can easily pick up the fine art of preventing your volunteers from acting.[2] Here's how.

- Laugh at the innovative ideas of others. Don't smirk. Use the full-fledged belly laugh.
- Take the idea you just laughed at and introduce it as your own approach.
- Give your volunteers lots of responsibility but no authority. Leave the impression in the larger congregation that your volunteers are actually overstepping their bounds of duty to assure that these workers are resented by others.
- Never say thanks or brag on others in public or spotlight the essential work of others in the church. No need to share the headlines, is there?
- Ignore the downcast nonverbals of your volunteers. It's probably just something they ate or a bad back or a mid-life crisis.
- Blame your volunteers when they become ineffective and finally drop out. Guilt added to apathy is a beautiful thing to observe.

Just to be sure you recognize real demotivation when you see it, here are some handy-dandy signs of honest-to-goodness demotivation: absenteeism, sloppy work, disloyalty, hostility, resistance to training, lateness for meetings.

Just in case you have one of those highly motivated volunteers who's almost impossible to keep from quality Christian service, here's the crowning demotivator: ignore him completely. Forget his name. Don't introduce him to others who come around. Gaze right through him like he's a picture window. When he makes a comment, act as if you don't hear him.

By concentrating on these easy principles, you too can become an accomplished demotivator. It's an essential skill for those of us who are forced to work with those pesky volunteers. Practice your basic doubt in human-kind, and you're already halfway to success!

Guidelines for Motivation in the Church

In a more serious vein, I like the statement attributed to Peter Drucker, the best known management theorist in America: "History has been written not by the most talented but by the most motivated!" Motivated Christians can write history. We can begin by improving the motivational climate of local churches.

Begin with the needs of members.

"Man is an ever-wanting animal," claimed Abraham Maslow. No one has highlighted the importance of needs in motivation better than Maslow in his famous "hierarchy of needs" model.[3] Maslow suggested that we are motivated by a number of basic needs. These fundamental needs can be rank ordered. Maslow depicted the most basic needs as body needs, then safety needs, followed by social needs, then esteem needs, and finally self-actualization needs. Your most basic unmet need consequently motivates you. When a need is satisfied, you automatically concentrate on the needs at the next higher level of the hierarchy.

An axiom has grown out of Maslow's ideas: a satisfied need isn't a motivator. If you want to help another church member feel motivated, help him discover his most basic unmet need and satisfy it. Sensitivity to other's real needs makes church leaders effective motivators.

Eliminate dissatisfiers.

Some factors irritate us and distract us from productive service. In churches these "hygiene factors,"[4] as they are called, range from hard pews to noisy teen-agers to long sermons. These items don't motivate us, but they encourage demotivation. (An analogy illustrates this principle. Garbage collection doesn't make us healthy; it does, however, help keep us from getting sick.) Dissatisfiers tend to relate to matters in our work environment and, therefore, can be more easily managed than the people around us.

Concentrate on the central motivators.

Research shows that five factors are central ingredients in motivation: achievement, recognition, the work itself, responsibility, and advancement. The content, then, of the service we are asked to provide through the church is crucial to our motivation. For example, an open process for developing clear goals helps us define achievement, which is one foundational motivator.

Encourage participation in church goal setting.

Volunteers (and others) take psychological ownership of the projects they create and plan. Involving the implementers in organizational goal setting, then, is motivational.

Create a motivational climate.

Persons who achieve in life tend to prefer an organizational setting with five specific ingredients.[5] (1) Explicit goals. (2) At least a fifty-fifty chance for success. (3) Feedback regarding their progress toward goals. (4) A high degree of individual responsibility and initiative. (5) A family-like atmosphere of support.

In a climate including these factors, productivity is likely. These principles can help you activate your congregation. Use them well to dispel inertia in your church.

XII

Traditionalists: Resisting the Challenge of Change

During the late nineteenth century the British Parliament debated closing the Royal Patent Office. Why? Some prominent Britons felt all significant inventions had already been discovered. According to this viewpoint, the process of change was slowing.

But change is a guaranteed phenomenon in our time, at least as sure as death and taxes. In response to the pervasiveness of change, some business schools now offer courses or training for manager trainees on how to guide change primarily. Their logic is if a leader can manage change, he has mastered the basic dynamic of world society today. An additional skill area, such as finance or personnel, gives a content focus for his change management work.

Change. It's everywhere! In fact, the future came yesterday, but most of us didn't notice. That's how fast life moves for us. When we sense the pace and pressure of change, we may resist change. Those of us in the church sometimes dig in our heels against change too. For example, for several years my ministry brought me into weekly contact with ministers in training seminars. In our conferences psychological tests were used for personal and professional growth purposes. As a result, I have group averages for roughly four hundred pastors. On a continuum measuring our responses to change, we scored 1.9 on a scale of ten, apparently quite change-resistant or traditional.

Traditionalists try to control their lives by slowing down the pace of change or by stopping it entirely. Who are some of the people who are apt to be change-resistant? Those who favor some "golden age" of their pasts. People with "old money." Those who fear personal obsolescence. People who are in power. And many others both in and beyond the church.

Finding the Traditionalist

Who is change-resistant? Have you seen these people in your congregation? The traditionalist is . . .

- Afraid of becoming obsolete.
- Someone who's in love with a past that never was and wants to prevent a future that never will be.
- A person who begins lots of sentences with "We used to . . ."
- An old "dog" who can't learn new tricks.
- Someone who has been burned by change previously.
- Moving ahead with the eyes on the rearview mirror.
- Not recognizing new possibilities.
- Fearful of the unknown.
- Comfortable with the way things are.
- Tied to tradition.
- Someone who knows all the answers.
- Unable to cope with new ideas.
- A person with low self-confidence.
- Someone longing for nostalgia.
- Anxious and insecure.

- Comfortable with the status quo.
- Someone whose grandfather started this church.
- A person who feels pushed.
- One who is comfortable with what's familiar.
- Fragile.
- A hardhead.
- Someone who structures his life so that he doesn't have to face change.
- A person who sees the past as a "golden age."
- An individual without vision.
- Someone who fears giants so much that he won't cross over into the Promised Land.
- The one who always says, "We never did it this way before."

Who Resists Change?

We resist change for lots of reasons. Our view of change and its meaning to us shapes our response to changes.

Creatures of habit—the passive resister.

We human beings become comfortable with our life routines. One of my favorite stories of the frontier relates to change. During the Gold Rush days of 1849, many wagon trains supplied themselves at St. Joseph, Missouri, before beginning their trek across the rutted prairie. Supposedly, this banner was strung across the western end of the street leading to the plains: "Choose your rut carefully. You may be in it all the way to California!"

The familiar becomes our rut—not because it's best, just because we've done that or been there before. "New" entices a few but triggers the anxieties in many more people. No wonder the seven last words of the church, according to some, is "We never did it this way before." Change resistance can be habit forming.

Recently a friend of mine told me a strangely familiar sounding story. He described how his family carefully plans and saves money all year for their summer vacation. Even after calculating the energy involved, the last few days before vacation are always a bit harried. Then, he claims, before the family car is filled with gear and about to clear the city limits on its way out-of-town, the "happy" family is fighting! Surprisingly, vacations are conflict occasions. They break our habit patterns and create havoc.

Without thinking, habits make us passive resisters of change. Our routine, like an old shoe, gets comfortable.

Appreciation of the past—the evolutionary change resisters.

History helps us understand how we got this way and discover our roots. We agree with Tevye that without traditions our lives become as unstable as a "fiddler on the roof." We easily become nostalgic about the "good old days." When confronted with change, we resist it unless it's the obvious, straight-line extension of our known past.

Bishop Pike initiated large-scale change by calling people back to "tradition." Even traditionalists find some change manageable when it's seen in a natural, evolutionary context.

Threatened by life's pace—the reactionary change resister.

Alvin Toffler's *Future Shock* expressed the feeling of psychological coma, which strikes us when we're overwhelmed by change. When change overruns us, we try desperately to hold life still. We plead, "Stop the world. I want to get off!" Threat creates an emotional resistance to change. It's amazing how change itself makes us reactionary and, therefore, more change resistant.

One of my seminary preaching professors insisted that his students put all their sermons into manuscript form. He spent ten years teaching the art of preaching and pressed us for full manuscripts consistently. Then he took a pastorate and invited me to lead a conference in his new church. Over lunch I asked him what he'd teach differently if he were back in the classroom again. His answer surprised me: "I'd stop insisting on manuscripted sermons. The pace of ministry tripled during the ten years I taught. I can't even get all of my own sermons into manuscript now. I use a full manuscript on Sunday morning, I develop an outline for Sunday evening, and I wing it on Wednesday evenings!" The pace of life pressures each of us into changes—some of them unwanted.

Injured by change—the revolutionary change resister.

If we feel we've been hurt by change, it becomes the enemy. This extreme response makes all change danger-ous, even revolutionary. Topsy-turvy change triggers irrational resistance, anger, distrust, overwhelming loss, withdrawal, and possibly violence.

These varied responses to change catch the church in the middle. Balance between change agentry and change resistance is difficult. We Christians value our heritage, yet we call for conversion and growth. We conserve our pasts while planning a new future. We are squeezed between tradition and change. Shall we simply record changes like a thermometer or cause change like a thermostat?

The Results of Extreme Change

While choices can be made about change, most of us react instinctively to change. And many of us resist extreme amounts of or rapidly paced change. Take this non-church case as an example, and you'll sense why the change resister in the church is no surprise.

Picture this. Two men are floating in a canoe on a fog-shrouded creek near the point in Montana where the Jefferson, Madison, and Gallatin rivers join to form the Missouri River. It's midsummer of 1809. It is also Blackfoot country—dangerous territory for two white men trapping beaver. The trappers are John Colter, the first mountain man, the first white man to see the Yellowstone Country and a veteran of the Lewis and Clark expedition, and his partner named Potts.

Colter and Potts are running their traps just before dawn when they hear a strange sound. Buffalo? No, it's Blackfeet, several hundred of them on both sides of the stream. The trappers beach their canoe, but Potts loses his composure and shoots an Indian. He, in return, is riddled with dozens of arrows and mutilated by the squaws and children.

Colter remains calm and defiant, although he knows well that his life is threatened too. The chiefs confer. One of them approaches Colter and asks, "Do you run fast?" Colter considers his lot and answers, "No, I run very slowly." Armed with that word, the chief returns to the parley. Then, Colter is instructed that he has a two-hundred-yard headstart in a race for his life. As Colter slowly walks to his advance point, he plots his strategy. His only chance, he decides, is to make a run for the Jefferson River six miles away. A chorus of war whoops begins the grim race.

Colter feels the agony of the run almost immediately. The Indians had stripped him of his boots and clothes. So the prickly pear spines bury themselves in his feet and lacerate his legs. Colter's lungs feel like they will burst. He becomes dizzy, his throat aches, waves of nausea hit him and his nose begins to bleed. Colter glances back and sees young Blackfoot runners scattered behind him across the plain. He realizes for the first time that he may have a chance. Run!

Exhaustion overtakes Colter. So does one fleet Blackfoot carrying an ugly spear. Colter stops and, in fear and weariness, screams at the young Indian closing in on him. The brave tries to stop, gather himself, and throw the spear in one motion. He only succeeds in burying his spear in the ground at Colter's feet. Colter grabs the weapon and kills the Indian. With a new burst of energy and optimism, Colter sets off again for the river now only a mile away.

When Colter arrives at the river, he dives in, swims under a beaver lodge, and hides silently for the rest of the day and night while the Blackfeet search for him. The next day Colter heads for Fort Lisa. Eleven days later he had covered the two hundred miles. Bloody, naked, cold, but alive—Colter had survived.

Colter attempted to trap in Blackfoot country again after recovering from his narrow escape. But another skirmish with Indians caused Colter to vow that if God would forgive him for coming to the West, he'd leave and never return. In 1810 Colter bought a small farm on the Missouri near St. Louis, married, and died in less than two years.

Physicians agree that massive change killed Colter. The physical and emotional stresses he faced took their toll. The pattern of intensity and respite, when carried to their extremes, creates a phenomenon called the "Colter coaster."[1] Rapid changes may make us sick or worse. It's no wonder change is resisted by many persons in our fast-paced world. Massive change can make traditionalists and change resisters of us.

But how can Christians understand change? Are there divine resources to stretch the traditionalist?

Convicting and Convincing

The Holy Spirit is a change agent in the Christian's life. Even our natural resistance to the new is confronted by the Holy Spirit. For instance, John 16:5-11 is considered by some commentators the best brief summary of the work of Holy Spirit of any single New Testament passage.

> It is to your advantage that I go away, for if I do not go away, the Counselor will not come to you; but if I go, I will send him to you. And when he comes, he will convince the world concerning sin and righteousness and judgment. (John 16:7b-8, RSV)

The word "convince" in English is the writer's term for the Holy Spirit's work. In Greek the word *elechein* suggests cross-examination in court or in a debate. A person is questioned until he admits his errors or acknowledges the correctness of some new point of view. *Elechein* has the force of both convicting of a wrong committed and convincing of the strength of a perspective rejected until now. The Holy Spirit is a powerful change agent—convicting and convincing us to change.

109

XIII

Congregations Cope with Change

A church is constantly coping with change. One variety of change a congregation must manage is personal adjustments.

When You're Overrun by Change

Future shock. Overload. Burnout. They're all words for the experience of feeling overrun by change. This experience is becoming almost commonplace in our culture.

For several years I've monitored my senior students' level of stress through the well-known Holmes and Rahe Life Change Scale. This scale indicates how much change a person has recently accumulated. Holmes and Rahe have ranked the most stressful changes humans undergo. They found, for instance, that the death of your spouse is the most traumatic change you experience. They assigned one hundred points to that change and, through testing with different age groups and in various cultures, they verified their ranking and the point values of their scale's forty-two events.

The Life Change Scale has a predictive quality to it. For example, an accumulation of 150 points or less projects a 37 percent chance of illness within the next two years, between 150 and 300 points pushes the odds of getting sick above 50 percent, and more than 300 points indicates an 80 percent chance of illness. About 25 percent of my students score in the lowest category, roughly 35 percent in the middle range, and nearly 40 percent in the highest and most dangerous level. Such high scores are a concern, particularly in a mobile group like graduating students.

Using the same Life Change Scale, apparently pastors accumulate almost three hundred points in a move from one church to another. Such a level places the new pastor in a stressful situation. But these health threats due to change aren't the exclusive problem of ministers. We're all susceptible to the pressures of change.

Adjusting to Personal Change

When we feel overrun by change (or fear we may be nearing a dangerous level of stress), we can take several helpful steps. We can help ourselves prevent some of the overload of change.

- Become familiar with life change events and the toll they take. This sensitivity will help you monitor the amount of stress you're undergoing.
- Pace yourself. We can get keyed up to dangerous levels. As one young man said, "Death is nature's way of telling us to slow down."
- When you reach a goal, consider it a happy part of the process of living. If we make an achievement a stopping point, we risk a dangerous ride on the "Colter coaster."
- Develop a support network. Friends who care about you and listen to you can help you become more aware of the stresses in life and manage them.

Congregational change is another vital type of change to be managed. Are there change enhancers, which help congregations make organizational adjustments more effectively?

Identifying an Organization's Change Enhancers

An array of factors creates a favorable climate for change in a church setting. Each of these items aids change. Taken together, these enhancers make organizational change much easier.

- Obvious need. If it's broken, it has to be fixed.
- Clear goals. When a direction is chosen, change energies are focused.
- Full and shared information. The facts—freely and completely offered—provide a foundation for consideration and action.
- Participative decision making. In congregational change efforts, everyone needs and deserves a say.
- Strong consensus. A meeting of the minds lends a launching pad for group change. Voting, on the other hand, may determine majority opinion but set opposition deeply enough to doom successful implementation of changes.
- Begin with healthy organizational components. Building a group's confidence in their attempts to change creates an atmosphere in which sicker groups and more resistant problems can be tackled.
- Stability in surrounding areas. Organizational change is enhanced by stability in adjoining areas of the organization. When the organization is generally shaky, change is harder to sell and to control.

- Exercise patience. Let time be your ally. Folks often resist the new until they've had a chance to digest the need for the change and the new facts related to it.
- Recognition of the grief aspect of change. Change causes loss. And loss triggers grief. Time to heal and regain our personal and organizational balance is vital after change occurs.

You can use these enhancers to plan increments of change. These factors are important resources in helping congregations develop.

Stages in Congregational Change

A pastor friend of mine claims change is a threatening idea for most congregations. So threatening that he says he no longer uses the word change in front of his church. Rather, he now talks about "development."

Can a comfortable change process for congregations be designed? How can congregations deal with the threat and necessity of changing or developing? A four-stage process can lend a structure for change.

Stage One: consciousness raising.

Nothing changes until people realize a challenge needs to be faced or a problem must be solved. Awareness of necessary adjustments begins with an "aha" experience. Cartoonists depict this event by drawing light bulbs above character's heads. Defining the problem shows your awareness has risen to a level where change will be considered.

113

Stage Two: increased understanding.

New information is usually needed for designing change processes. In local churches the information required for change usually means more than sermons, study committees, Sunday school lessons, and bulletin boards. These vehicles provide some information, but knowing something doesn't mean automatic change.

New information calls for an integration with old information. That is, before we can make changes we must make the new and old mesh comfortably. Old ways of coping are updated with the fresh approaches.

Stage Three: personal empowerment.

When a need is identified and the required information is mastered, a sense of power grows. Now there's the ability to respond, a slightly different flavor to responsibility (response-ability). Knowing you understand how to tackle a problem gives you leverage on needed changes.

Stage Four: congregational implementation.

Making change is now the only step left. To make the needed adjustments, a congregational process must be developed for (1) exploring alternatives, (2) reaching a congregational consensus, (3) assuming ownership for both personal and corporate responsibilities, (4) adjusting the organization and practicing the changes, (5) allowing the congregation to recover its equilibrium, and, (6) celebrating the successful implementation of changes.

Planned organizational change has a political flavor for some church members. Does it for you?

Politics in the Church

Wheeling and dealing. Shady. Manipulative. Smoke-filled rooms. These unfavorable images describe our popular view of politics. In some cases, politics can be unsavory business.

Does politics have any place in the church? Not using the tactics mentioned above! But, originally politics referred to "polis," meaning city or people. In that sense, the church is inevitably a political institution. After all, the church is people. Ministry is people at work and builds on relationships between persons. Therefore, church leaders have a political dimension in their work. That dimension is not good or bad inherently. Politics in the church is just a reality. As long as the church is basically people and difficult members exert control on the mission of the congregation, politics will remain one facet of church leadership.

Two additional dimensions of change management—cultural and national change—face local congregations too. Is your church making plans on the local level to deal creatively with these broader, longer-term changes?

Anticipated Global Changes

In 1977 President Carter called for a study of the probable changes in the world by the year 2000. The result was the "Global 2000 Report," a chilling reminder of changes in the world we are creating.[1] Here are some of the report's predictions:

- *More people*. A one-third increase in world population is projected during the final twenty-five years of this

115

century. Four hundred cities are projected to have one million residents by 2000.

- *Richer rich people and poorer poor people.* The industrialized nations of the world will exceed $11,000 in per capita gross national product while the less developed countries will stay below $600.
- *War over water.* World demand for water will double or triple by the end of the century. Since three-fourths of the world's rivers are shared by two nations and the remaining one-fourth provide borders for three to ten nations, it is easy to see that water means survival and may figure in future wars.
- *Wood, the poor man's oil.* One-half of the world's accessible timber will be cut by the year 2000. In some of the less developed countries, one family member is already forced to gather fuel wood full-time.
- *Poor food distribution.* Although food supplies are expected to increase by 90 percent before 2000, malnourished humans will triple in number to a total of 1.3 billion by the end of this century. The practical result? The children of the poorest of the poor will never reach normal body weight or intelligence.
- *Spreading deserts.* Erosion (caused by overgrazing, destructive cropping practices, and burning stalks and animal dung for fuel) will remove several inches of topsoil from the world's croplands by the turn of the century. Across the globe every year an area roughly the size of Indiana or South Carolina will become additional desert.
- *Energy appetite.* This issue is considered so unpredictable the report only suggests that energy consumption will expand in every sector of the globe and energy will cost much more.

The writers of the "Global 2000 Report" didn't factor wars or interruptions of world trade patterns into their projections. Whatever else this report says to Christians, global change must be faced beginning in local churches.

How the United States Is Changing

How familiar are you with changes happening in our own country? Let me give you a pop quiz.

1. During the decade of the 1970s more than 40 percent of American population growth occurred in only three states. Can you name them?
2. Which region of the United States has the highest percentage of college and high school trained persons?
3. Which state has replaced Connecticut as the highest per capita income state in our country?
4. Which region of the United States has represented home territory for the last four elected American presidents?

Let's "score" your answers. (1) California, Texas, and Florida, all Sunbelt states, are setting the pace in population growth. (2) The West has the best-educated population. (3) Alaska is now the most affluent state in the union. (4) The Sunbelt has produced our recent presidents.

The general shift of people, industry, and influence from the Northeast to the South and West is only one of the "megatrends" currently changing America.[2] These trends call on congregations to respond to change and aggressively shape our ministry to the new nation, which is rapidly emerging.

117

Who Decides?

Someone will control the changes your congregation faces. Traditionalists, for a variety of reasons, will resist change. Progressives, also acting from a range of motives, will advocate change. Can you develop a consensus to advance the kingdom of God? That's the goal of Christians anyway.

XIV

Not an Endangered Species

Difficult church members are not an endangered species. The lonely, cliques, crazymakers, hostiles, the apathetic, and traditionalists are here to stay in the church. Neither are we as church leaders to put them on an endangered species list and eradicate them. Positively, we hope to recognize, understand, and minister to them redemptively. We can learn from working with difficult members because, according to the proverb, "A smooth sea never made a skillful mariner." On the negative side, we want to survive these difficult church members' attempts to control us and the congregation.

A Ministry Strategy

A general strategy for ministry to difficult church members is suggested by our identification and exploration of these six types.

- Accept the difficult member as a person of worth. However, you don't have to approve of his controlling tactics.
- Establish an open relationship with difficult members and keep it current. Know what's going on in the lives of the difficult members of your congregation.

- Try to see life in the church from their viewpoint. Learn to recognize and understand their patterns of behavior.
- Look for legitimate ways to meet their needs without hindering the congregation or draining your own energies.
- Work behind the scenes with difficult members. If difficulties can be dealt with behind the scenes, the entire congregation is spared stress and strain.

No member of Christ's church, no matter how difficult, stands beyond the covenant to care. Love and concern are antidotes for the controlling behaviors of difficult members. Selective love is not in the Christian vocabulary. When the covenant to care binds us together, we can form a world-changing band. The last word, after all, is covenant.

Last Word . . . and Testament

Covenant. That's the last word. A solemn promise. A binding pledge. A testament. There is an implied covenant in the church that we will care for each other, warts and all. Difficult members are included in this covenant too. Our common commitment to Jesus Christ binds us together more closely than our different personalities wedge us apart.

Take Jesus' apostle band as one illustration of a group in covenant. A more diverse group would be hard to imagine. A radical politician: Simon the Zealot. A turncoat tax collector: Matthew. An impulsive leader: Simon Peter. A behind-the-scenes evangelist: Andrew. Two ambitious, hotheaded brothers: James and John. The eventual betrayer: Judas. And several others from differing backgrounds and outlooks. What a mixture!

After Jesus' death and resurrection, however, this range of personalities became of team of world-changing missionaries. If they were not sure before, they then realized the power of a mutual vision of the kingdom of God. Their differences enriched their band and unified their bond. They were in covenant and on mission.

Notes

Chapter I

1. Robert M. Bramson, *Coping with Difficult People* (Garden City, N.Y.: Anchor Press, 1981), p. 6.

Chapter II

1. Alfred North Whitehead, *Religion in the Making* (New York: Macmillan Publishing Co., 1954), pp. 16-17.
2. Velma Darbo Stevens, *A Fresh Look at Loneliness* (Nashville: Broadman Press, 1981), p. 26.
3. James J. Lynch, *The Broken Heart: the Medical Consequences of Loneliness* (New York: Basic Books, Publishers, 1977), p. xiii.

Chapter III

1. Robert S. Weiss, *Loneliness: the Experience of Emotional and Social Isolation* (Cambridge, Mass.: Massachusetts Institute of Technology Press, 1973), pp. 9-27.
2. John Hritzuk, *The Silent Company: How to Deal with Loneliness* (New York: Spectrum, 1982).

3. Marney Rich, "Social Worker Offers a Hand to the Needy," *Raleigh (NC) News & Observer*, 24 January 1982, pp. 1-III and 2-III.
4. Nell Perry, "Secrets: What You Don't Tell Can Hurt You," *Raleigh (NC) Times*, 1 December 1977, p. 1-B.
5. Margery Williams, *The Velveteen Rabbit* (Garden City, N.Y.: Doubleday & Co., 1958), p. 17.

Chapter IV

1. Wayne Oates, *Pastoral Counseling in Social Problems* (Philadelphia: Westminster Press, 1966), pp. 36-56.

Chapter V

1. Clyde Reid, *Groups Alive—Church Alive* (New York: Harper & Row, Publishers, 1969), pp. 61-75.
2. Kurt Lewin, *Resolving Social Conflicts* (New York: Harper & Brothers, 1948).

Chapter VI

1. George Bach and Yetta M. Bernhard, *Aggression Lab* (Dubuque, Iowa: Kendall/Hunt Publishing Co., 1971), pp. 193-200.

Chapter VII

1. Gerard I. Nierenberg and Henry H. Calero, *Meta-talk* (New York: Trident Press, 1973).

Chapter VIII

1. Ronald H. Bailey, *Violence and Aggression* (Alexandria, Va.: Time-Life Books, 1976).

Chapter X

1. John Savage, *The Apathetic & Bored Church Member*, (Pittsford, N.Y.: LEAD Consultants, 1976).
2. "Hey, Nobody, Somebody Loves You," *Raleigh (NC) Times*, 5 November 1979.
3. Richard Restak, *The Self-Seekers* (New York: Doubleday & Co., 1982).

Chapter XI

1. Harvey Cox, *God's Revolution and Man's Responsibility* (Valley Forge, PA: Judson Press, 1965), pp. 39-49.
2. Norma Ederer, "Nine Easy Ways to Demotivate Employees," *Training/HRD*, August, 1979, p. 83.
3. For Abraham Maslow's theories of motivation, see *Motivation and Personality*, 2nd ed. (New York: Harper & Row, 1970) and *Toward a Psychology of Being* (Princeton, N.J.: Van Nostrand Reinhold Co., 1968).
4. The motivation-hygiene theory was developed by Frederick Herzberg. His ideas on motivation are explored in his books *Motivation to Work*, 2nd ed., (New York: John Wiley & Sons, 1959) and *Work and the Nature of Man* (New York: World Publishing, 1966).
5. David McClelland, *The Achieving Society* (New York: Free Press, 1961).

Chapter XII

1. Donald L. Dudley and Elton Welke, *How to Survive Being Alive* (Garden City, N.Y.: Doubleday & Co., 1977), pp. 10-90.

Chapter XIII

1. Gerald O. Barney, *The Global Two Thousand Report to the President of the U.S.*, 3 vols. (Washington, D.C.: U.S. Government Printing Office, 1980).
2. John Naisbitt, *Megatrends: Ten New Directions Transforming Our Lives* (New York: Warner Books, 1982).